Red-Tailed Boas

Ben Aller, Mark K. Bayless,
and Riley Campbell

Red-Tailed Boas

Project Team
Editors: Thomas Mazorlig and Adam Black
Copy Editor: Mary Grangeia
Cover Design: Mary Ann Kahn
Interior Design: Mary Ann Kahn

T.F.H. Publications
President/CEO: Glen S. Axelrod
Executive Vice President: Mark E. Johnson
Publisher: Christopher T. Reggio
Production Manager: Kathy Bontz

T.F.H. Publications, Inc.
One TFH Plaza
Third and Union Avenues
Neptune City, NJ 07753

Printed and bound in China,
07 08 09 10   3 5 7 9 8 6 4 2
ISBN 978-0-79382888-3

Library of Congress Cataloging-in-Publication Data
Aller, Ben.
Red-tailed boas : a complete guide to Boa constrictor / Ben Aller and Mark K. Bayless.
p. cm.
Includes bibliographical references and index.
ISBN 0-7938-2888-0 (alk. paper)
1. Boa constrictors as pets. I. Bayless, Mark K. II. Title.
SF459.S5A45 2006
639.3'967--dc22
2005036194

The Leader In Responsible Animal Care For Over 50 Years!™
www.tfhpublications.com

Table of Contents

The red-tailed boa (often called the boa constrictor or just the boa) has been kept as a pet in households all over North, Central, and South America for centuries. Some people have ascribed magical powers to these snakes and others have kept them in 19th century New York City apartments under gaslight heat. Conquistador Hernan Cortes believed the boa constrictor to be an insidious snake that caused the death of both animal and man alike by impalement with its red-tipped tail! This is obviously not true, and the red-saddled tail is harmless. However, many misconceptions about boas persist. This book will reveal the true nature of this beautiful snake and how to properly keep it as a pet and even breed it.

The first real book on the husbandry of exotic reptiles was written by E.G. Boulenger, son of esteemed Georges Boulenger, Curator of Amphibians, Reptiles and Fishes at the British Museum in London and was published in 1896. In the last 100 years, we've come a long way in terms of offering red-tailed boas and other reptiles better and better care in captivity. As we begin the 21st century, the knowledge gained

Introduction

and the improvements we have made in the husbandry of reptiles and amphibians has led to a surge in captive breeding and increased popularity in the pet trade of this much maligned snake.

The red-tailed boa is one of the most widespread snakes of the Americas, ranging from the Sonora Desert in northern Mexico to the grasslands of Argentina, from the shores of the Caribbean and Atlantic Oceans in the east to the Pacific Ocean in the west. It is a most adaptable reptile. The adaptability of this snake is reflected in the ways this animal is kept in captivity as well, as it will survive—although not necessarily thrive—in many different types of terraria. The variety and amount of prey this snake can ingest is amazing, and so is its size, ranging from three feet (0.9 m) total length for some island varieties to nearly 15 feet (4.6 m) in length for rainforest forms.

In the following pages, you will learn how to live with, enjoy, and maintain one of nature's most marvelous and enjoyable reptiles. Many of the questions and answers you need to know are within these pages, and we certainly hope you and your snake have a happy and healthy time together.

Chapter 1

Natural History

While you may think of your red-tailed boa as a pet, it is essentially a wild animal. Even a captive-bred boa is still only a few generations removed from the wild, and it has all the needs and instincts of its wild cousins. To better understand your boa, you will need to understand something of its habitat and behavior in nature.

Red-Tails at a Glance

Red-tailed boas are one of the most popular pet snakes. There are a number of reasons for this, including their beautiful colors and patterns, their (mostly) docile temperament, their large—but not unmanageable—size, and their hardiness. But what exactly is a red-tailed boa?

Red-tailed boas are large snakes that range from warm temperate to tropical climates in Central and South America. They belong to a large family of snakes commonly called boas, and the family is known scientifically as Boidae. All boas are nonvenomous and kill their prey by constricting it with their body. Unlike most other snakes, boas give birth to live young. Red-tailed boas typically reach an adult size of 9 feet (2.7 m), although the size varies widely by geographic origin, subspecies, individual, and keeping conditions.

Because they vary so much, coming up with a general description of a red-tailed boa is difficult. In general, red-tails are brownish gray snakes with a triangle-shaped head set off sharply from the neck. Most have black speckling. A dark brown stripe runs from the tip of the nose down the back of the head to the neck. Another stripe runs through each eye. On the back, there are 15 to 30 hourglass-shaped saddles. These often contain

Red-tailed boas have an enormous natural range and can be found in a diverse array of habitats, from rainforests to deserts.

Table 1: Key to Boa Constrictor Subspecies
(Peters, 1970, 1986; Langhammer, 1983)

1. Conspicuous dorsal pattern always present: . . . . .go to 2
   Dorsal pattern pale or dark, but always inconspicuous
   or even absent: . . . . go to 5

2. Longitudinal middorsal band on head without lateral projections: . . . .go to 3
   Longitudinal middorsal band on head sends lateral
   projections to eyes: . . . . .B. c. imperator

3. Dorsal pattern of yellow spots bordered by black rings
   which are connected to each other: . . . . .go to 4
   Black rings around yellow dorsal spots not in contact
   with one another: . . . . .B. c. occidentalis

4. More than 21 saddle-shaped dorsal spots; ventral scales
   226-237, pale color, high number of saddles: . . . . .B.c. amarali
   Fewer than 20 rounded dorsal spots;
   234-250 ventral scales: . . . . .B.c constrictor
   Two large spots in the infralabial region on
   each side; ventral scales 258-259: . . . . .B.c. sigma (no longer recognized)

5. Dorsal color pale, light, sandy: . . . . .B.c. ortonii
   Dorsal color dark reddish brown: . . . . .B.c. sabogae
   Dark ventral belly: . . . . .B.c. melanogaster

short, pale bars at the point where the snake's back becomes its side. On the lower side and between the saddles are brown, vaguely diamond-shaped blotches that usually have pale centers. The saddles on the tail become larger and, as the common name suggests, are reddish in color. The red ranges from mostly brown to bright scarlet. The spaces between the red saddles are cream-colored to white. The boas with the brightest red tails are generally the most sought after.

Range and Habitat

The red-tailed boa has an enormous natural range; it is the largest of any reptile in the New World. It ranges from Sonora and Tamaulipas in Mexico, south along both coastlines

Scientific Names

Biologists determine the scientific name of each animal based on what other animals it is related to. Each scientific name has two parts: The first part of the name is called the genus, while the second part is the species. This combination of genus and species is unique for each animal. Scientific names allow scientists all over the world to talk about an animal without similar animals being confused with the one they want to discuss. A scientific name is often abbreviated after the first usage. The genus is abbreviated to the first letter. So, after introducing the red-tailed boa as *Boa constrictor* it can be referred to as *B. constrictor*. If the author is talking about all the snakes in this genus, he or she can use boa without a species name attached. Some animals have a third name, which indicates that it is a subspecies. Subspecies describe different varieties that exist within a species, such as the Argentine boa, *Boa constrictor occidentalis.*

throughout much of Central and South America (east of the Andes), and to central Argentina and Paraguay. There is some conjecture that the boa might have ranged into southwestern Arizona in the recent past (Allen, 1933; Taylor, 1936; Bogert, 1945). If this is true, the boa subspecies would range from the southwestern United States to Argentina! That is an amazing amount of territory for a single species to cover.

It appears that habitat is not as important to the *Boa constrictor* as the temperature range within the habitat. From Sonora, Mexico, 150 miles south of Arizona's border, to northern Argentina, the red-tailed boas live in various habitats but maintain an optimal body temperature range, regardless of whether an individual dwells in a hot desert, a warm and muggy forest on the equator, or in a cooler scrubland of Peru's highlands (Pope, 1961). The species has even been found in Venezuela's Andean mountain range (Casado, 1996). As long as the habitat supplies the necessary temperature range and opportunities to control their body temperature, boas may thrive there.

Boas inhabit an amazing variety of environments across their massive distribution range. They may be found from sea level to 3,000 feet (914 m) above sea level in wet and dry tropical savannahs, very dry thorn scrubs, and adjacent to and in cultivated fields. They are crepuscular (nocturnal), secretive animals and are able to maintain preferred body temperatures without basking outright, as many lizards and other snakes must do.

Taxonomy

Taxonomy is the scientific system of naming, ranking, and classifying organisms. Modern taxonomy is a system by which plants and animals are recognized and named today in an organization called *binomial nomenclature*. In this system, animals are assigned a genus (plural: genera) and a species name. Genera denote animals of the same affinity within a larger category called a family. Species is a name given to each distinct member of the genera. Therefore, each animal and plant has a genus-species name, called the *scientific name*. Some animals, including the boa constrictor, have a third name that denotes the subspecies. Subspecies are recognized when there are populations of a species that are different than others but not so different that they should be considered a true species. The scientific name of the red-tailed boa is *Boa constrictor*.

Boa constrictors are classified in the family Boidae, commonly called the "true boas." A true boa can simply be described as follows: Its body is more or less compressed; its head is distinct from the neck, with a squared muzzle; its pupils are oblong and erect; its teeth are larger in the front than in the rear of its mouth; and its tail is prehensile.

There are a number of different subspecies of the red-tailed boa. This is the Argentine boa, *Boa constrictor occidentalis*.

A spur is present on each side of the cloaca, the common opening for waste elimination and reproduction. These claws are the remnants from when the ancestors of today's boas had legs millions of years ago. These leg remnants and some other features have made scientists consider the boas a primitive family of snakes. Boas differ from other neotropical snakes in that they have shiny, smooth scales, 55 or more rows of mid-body scales, and no enlarged plate-like scales on the top or sides of the head. The other South American members of the family Boidae are the tree boas (genus *Corallus*), rainbow and slender boas (genus *Epicrates*), and the anacondas (genus *Eunectes*).

Although largely found in the Americas, true boas can also be found on Madagascar and some South Pacific islands. If you consider the sand boas to be true boas, then they are also found in western and central Asia, northern Africa, and southern Europe. Boas differ from

Scale Terms

Many of the scales on a snake have names used by scientists and other professionals to facilitate discussions of snake anatomy, taxonomy, and other subjects. A partial glossary of these named scales is below.

anal: Scale that covers the vent.

frontal: Scale on top of the head, between the eyes; broken into many small scales in boas.

infralabials: Scales on the lower "lip" (although snakes don't really have lips).

internasals: Scales on top of the head between the nostrils; small and fragmented in boas.

nasals: Scale or scales on the side of the head surrounding (at least partially) the nostril.

postoculars: Scale or scales on the side of the head behind the eye.

preoculars: Scales on the sides of the head in front of the eyes.

rostral: Scale on the tip of the snout.

subcaudals: Scales on the undersurface of the tail. Males have more than females.

supralabials: Scales on the upper "lip."

supraoculars: Scales directly above the eye.

ventrals: Scales on the belly.

the superficially similar pythons in that they bear live young rather than depositing eggs, lack teeth on the premaxillary bone, and lack the postfrontal bone in the skull; pythons lay eggs, have teeth on the premaxillary bone, and have a postfrontal bone.

Subspecies and Other Varieties

Because *Boa constrictor* has such a large natural range and has adapted to many different habitats, there are many variations in its physical form. Some of these are more consistent and different than others. Many of these variations are considered subspecies, while others are just considered interesting forms of one of the subspecies.

Depending on whom you consult, there are anywhere from 8 to 15 recognized subspecies of *Boa constrictor* that exist in the wild (Forcart, 1951; Peters, 1986; Barker, 1994; Schatzl, 1995). Tables 1 through 5 give a summation of the complex taxonomy and distribution. It is possible that some of these subspecies are actually distinct species, but it is also possible that these subspecies just represent a gradual change in appearance over the range (called a *cline* by biologists).

Boa constrictor constrictor

This subspecies is usually found under the names boa constrictor and red-tailed boa. In fact, when hobbyists use the whole phrase "red-tailed boa" they are normally talking

Table 2: The Ranges of the Boa Constrictor Subspecies

Subspecies	Range
Boa constrictor constrictor	Venezuela and Columbia to S. Brazil
Boa constrictor amarali	S. Brazil, E. Bolivia, Paraguay
Boa constrictor imperator	Mexico, Central America, W. Columbia, Ecuador, many off-shore islands, introduced in Florida
Boa constrictor longicauda	Tumbes Province, Peru
Boa constrictor melanogaster	Ecuador
Boa constrictor nebulosus	Dominica, West Indies
Boa constrictor occidentalis	Argentina and Paraguay
Boa constrictor orophias	Trinidad, St. Lucia, Dominica, St. Kitts
Boa constrictor ortonii	Chilette, Peru
Boa constrictor sabogae	Taboga Island, Panama

about this subspecies. When talking about this subspecies, the country of origin is often included, so you may see a price list showing Brazilian red-tailed boas, Guyanan red-tailed boas, and Surinam red-tailed boas.

It is the second-most popular subspecies in the hobby. Hobbyists sometimes refer to this subspecies by the acronym BCC, which is derived from the first letter of the genus, species, and subspecies names.

The original description of *Boa constrictor constrictor* provided by Carl Linnaeus in 1758 is brief, with India incorrectly given as its locality. The boa constrictor illustrates a rare instance in which an animal has the same scientific name as its common name (another example is the western gorilla: *Gorilla gorilla*). It has a slightly prominent snout. Its ventral scales range from 234-243, with 15-22 rather neat geometric dorsal saddles from the head to the cloaca. The dorsal ground color is a fawn-brown to a tan-beige or yellowish color. The ventral side of the body is light colored, with a white or yellow hue. In several populations of this subspecies, the red tail saddles are particularly vibrant.

This subspecies has a large natural range. It is found over much of South America east of the Andes and north of Argentina and Paraguay. The range includes the countries of (north to south) Columbia (eastern), Venezuela, Guyana, Surinam, French Guiana, Brazil, Ecuador (eastern), Peru (eastern), and Bolivia (northern). It is found on many islands off the coast of South America, including Trinidad and Tobago.

The boa subspecies *B. c. constrictor* is often called the "true" red-tailed boa. This beautiful one was found in Brazil.

Boa constrictor amarali

Amaral's boa is not common in the reptile trade. It also goes under the names Bolivian boa, short-tailed boa, and spectacled boa.

The range of the subspecies lies between that of *Boa constrictor constrictor* in the north and that of the Argentine boa (*Boa constrictor occidentalis*) in the south. It occurs from southeast Bolivia through Paraguay's wooded Parana Plateau and into Brazil across the southern regions of Mato Grosso do Sur and Goias into Sao Paulo State. It is not clear where *B. c. amarali* and *B. c. occidentalis* overlap in range in northern Argentina. This subspecies inhabits savannas, woodlands, and the southern Atlantic forest of southern Brazil, eastern Paraguay, and the forested, swampy Pantanal region along the eastern Bolivian border at the eastern slopes of the Andes.

B. c. amarali is distinguished from other subspecies as follows: It has a dorsal scale count from 71 to 79; the ventral scale count is 226 to 237; the subcaudal scale averages 43-52 scales; and it is grayer and lighter in color than other subspecies. The most conspicuous feature that distinguishes this species from the others is its pale background color and sometimes dark red or dark maroon saddles seen on the tail (Barker, 1994). The tail is considered by some to be shorter than that of other subspecies (Stull, 1932; Barker, 1994). In 1980, late reptile breeder Lloyd Lemke described this boa subspecies as follows: "*Boa constrictor amarali* are colored basic shades of grey or brown, with indistinct ground color saddles. Their tails are very short and stubby, with either no or little red on them. Their ventral sides are a grey/black/pink collage similar to that seen in *B. c. occidentalis* (Lemke, pers. com.).

This subspecies in Brazil lives in moist habitats, such as riverbanks, plantations, and rain forests throughout its range. Amaral's boas feed on tree porcupines, which inhabit mainly tropical evergreen forest; however, these boas sometimes can be found in dry deciduous forest in the vicinity of streams.

Scale Counts

Some of the characteristics of snakes that herpetologists use for species identification are the scale counts, the numbers of different types of scales. The three most commonly used are the dorsal scale rows, the ventrals, and the subcaudals. The dorsals are counted at the mid-body in either a zigzag row around the body or in a continuous oblique row forward to the central scale over the center of the back and then backward down the other side (in a chevron when viewed from above). The ventral count is the number of scales on the undersurface of the body, not including the anal scale or the scales of the tail. The subcaudal count is just the number of scales on the undersurface of the tail.

It is difficult to get accurate scale counts on live animals. They sometimes can be obtained from a shed skin. Sometimes when snakes are bred for generations in captivity, the scale counts begin to diverge from the normal for the species, probably an artifact of the limited gene pool.

Boa constrictor imperator

This is the subspecies most commonly found in the pet trade. It is farmed and exported from several countries, most notably Columbia. It is often sold under the names Central American boa, Columbian boa, Mexican boa, northern boa constrictor. A healthy B. c. *imperator* is often more iridescent than the other subspecies. As with B. c. *constrictor*, hobbyists often refer to this subspecies by the initials of its scientific name, BCI.

One of the widest ranging subspecies, the Central American boa occurs from northern Mexico south over all of Central America and into northwestern South America. In South America it inhabits western Columbia and the northwestern third of Ecuador. During the early 20th century, herpetologists knew of reports that this subspecies occurred in southern Arizona as well (Bogert, 1945; Pope, 1961), but to date no verified specimens have been discovered there. The most northern locality for this subspecies comes from Tetuchie (sometimes spelled Tetuachi) in Sonora, Mexico, approximately 750 meters (2461 ft) above sea level on June 7, 1979.

Boa constrictor imperator is the only boa subspecies found north of South America. This makes identification in the field easy, but it does not help in the pet trade. Central American boas have 22-30 dorsal saddles, which is a higher count than B. c. *constrictor* has, which is the

In-Between Boa

Herpetologist Olive Stull believed Amaral's boa to be an intermediate form between *Boa constrictor constrictor* and *Boa constrictor occidentalis* in appearance and geographical range (Stull, 1932). The subspecies was first collected at Sao Paulo, Brazil by Dr. Afranio do Amaral (1894-1982). It was named in his honor by Stull in

subspecies the Central American boa is most likely to be confused with. It also has 55-79 dorsal scales and 225-259 ventrals. Additionally, Central American boas are almost never as colorful as the nominate subspecies.

A pale, dwarfed form of B. c. *imperator* from islands off of Honduras is called the Hog Island boa, and it is bred by hobbyists and professional snake breeders. However, this type of boa can also be found on the mainland, which demonstrates how confusing some of the names in the pet trade can be. Populations of this subspecies may be found on other off-shore islands in Central America.

This subspecies has a large natural range and is found in many different habitats, from the interior of an extinct volcano (at La Playa, Jorullo Volcano, Michoacan, Mexico) to sea caves on Providencia Island, 124 miles (200 km) off the coast of Nicaragua. It is found in dry forests, savannahs and deserts but is also found in wetter climates, even among coastal red mangrove swamps.

In the foothills of the Sierra Madre of northwestern Mexico, boa constrictors could be found at approximately 825 feet (250 m) above sea level, 75 miles (120.7 km) west of the Gulf of California, which consists of deciduous (woody) thorn scrub. Temperatures as low as 51.8°F (11°C) have been recorded for this region in December. This subspecies is able to survive in almost temperate climates.

Some herpetologists believe this subspecies is more arboreal than other boa constrictors. In Belize, this species has been found

Amaral's boa is a dark-tailed subspecies found in Paraguay, Bolivia, and southern Brazil.

Table 3. Body Temperatures of Boa Constrictors

Total Length (inches/cm)	Air Temperature	Surface Temperature	Body Temperature	Source
78.8/200	72.6°F (22.6 C}	76°F (24.4°C)	86.7°F (30.4°C)	Myres (1968)
50.4/128	72.6°F (22.6°C)	76°F (24.4°C)	88°F (31°C)	Myres (1968)
49.6/126	72.6°F (22.6°C)	76°F (24.4°C)	88°F (31°C)	Myres (1968)
46.4/119	72.6 (22.6°C)	76°F (24.4°C)	87°F (30.5°C)	Myres (1968)
42.5/108	75.2°F (24°C)	72.5°F (22.5°C)	78.4°F (25.8°C)	Myers (1968)
31.2/79.2	74-83°F (23.3-28.3°C)	75°F (23.9°C)	76-85°F (24.4-29.4°C)	Montgomery (1978)
15-20/38-51	101°F (38.5°C)	122°F (50°C)	87-92°F (24.4-29.4°C)	McGinnis (1969)

The five snakes discovered by Myres were found on a rock-gravel substrate at the mouth of a denning cavity. They were folded against one another laterally, exposing a maximum amount of their bodies toward the sun. No snake was coiled on top of another snake. The five boa constrictors observed in Table 6 cooled much slower when aggregative than they did when individually. Hence, aggregation is a distinct behavioral advantage to them when the sun is out but the ambient air temperature is cool.

high in trees, and in Cays among optimum habitats in red mangrove swamps. Typically, lowland boas are darker in color, but in the red mangrove swamps of the Cays, they also have a reddish color to them. Dr. Wilfred Neill has noted that reptiles and amphibians that inhabit red mangrove stands are often reddish in color, and it appears mangrove-dwelling boas are not different (Neill, 1958).

Boa constrictor longicauda

This subspecies of boa constrictor is the most recently recognized member of the boa complex. It was described from a boa population located east of Tumbles Province in Peru. The first specimen was collected on June 14, 1988 and described in 1991.

The name *longicauda* actually means "long tailed," and hobbyists usually refer to this boa as the long-tailed boa. This is not a bad name for the animal, since it differs from other subspecies in having a longer tail, especially the males. On average, the tail is 14.1 percent longer than other subspecies. Long-tailed boas are rarities in the hobby, but there are some breeders working with them.

This subspecies has fewer saddle blotches (21-22) than B. c. imperator, a longitudinal mid-dorsal band without projections to the eyes, and a darker head and body coloration, without red or tan color on the tail in adults. It differs from B. c. constrictor in that it lacks red on the tail and has few mid-body scale rows (81-76), and a black spotted head pattern. B. c. longicauda is darker overall than B. c. ortonii, lacks its red tail color, and has a lower ventral count of 223-247 (B. c. ortonii has 246-252). Finally, it differs from B. c. melanogaster in that it has a much longer tail, lacks the black ventral surface, has fewer dorsal scales, and from B. c. occidentalis in that it has an entirely different color and pattern.

Boa constrictor longicauda's closest relative is probably B. c. imperator, as their scale counts are similar and their ranges so close together. The subspecies is known from the Tumbes

Island Hoppers

There are continued island expansions in the distribution of *Boa constrictor imperator* among coastal islands. For example, in 1971, six boa constrictors were deposited on Cozumel Island (Martinez-Morales, 1999), which, like most islands, has few predators, so the snakes were able to populate the island quickly. In April 1969, boas were first seen on Aruba Island, and by December of 1973, there were a reported 273 boas ranging in size from neonates to adults measuring 8 feet (2.8 meters) (Quick, 2005).

On Cozumel Island, Mexico, two to six boa constrictors were introduced to the 486 square-kilometer oceanic island in 1971 for the making of the Mexican film, "El Jardin de Tia Isabe." More than 75 percent of this island is covered with tropical semi-deciduous forest, low lying tropical deciduous forest, and mangrove swamps. Nearly 30 years after their introduction to this island, the boa constrictor is now widespread there (Martinez-Morales, 1999).

It is quite probable that precolumbian peoples moved the boas around, as well. Other snakes are known to swim and raft over to islands, so boas have probably done the same.

The most common subspecies of red-tailed boa in the pet trade is *B. c. imperator*, the Central American boa.

Province of Peru, a region that is a wet tropical refuge surrounded to the north, east, and south by a cordillera rising 1,863 miles (3,000 km) high (Price, 1991).

Boa constrictor melanogaster

James K. Langhammer of the Detroit Zoological Park first described this subspecies in 1983. It was a female collected by a Jivaro Indian in December of 1968 near Rio Yaupi Catholic Mission in the Morona Santiago Province of Ecuador. The validity of this subspecies is questionable, and it is extremely rare in the hobby.

Boa constrictor melanogaster has a deep mahogany-colored red tail. This subspecies also has a black ventral color, which distinguishes it from the other species/subspecies of boa constrictors discussed here. It has the smallest number of caudal scales ranging from 86-94, and ventral scutes measuring 244 scales. The dorsal saddles are usually bordered by black (Langhammer, 1983). It is usually called the black-bellied boa.

This subspecies' range is at the convergence of two rivers in Ecuador, the Rio Yaupi and the Rio Santiago in the Morona Santiago Province (Langhammer, 1983). The Amazonian jungles of eastern Ecuador are still vastly unexplored, however, so little else is known about this subspecies or its habitat.

Boa constrictor nebulosa

This subspecies is an insular (island) form known from Dominica Island in the West Indies (Lazell, 1964; Henderson, 2003). It is usually called the clouded or Dominican boa. It is rare in the hobby, but is being bred by a few herpetoculturists in Germany.

This subspecies is said to have a strikingly convex canthus (nose), a dark, clouded, grey-brown color, with a venter from ash to slate grey. Both loreal and subocular stripes are absent. Like other insular reptiles known to tropical islands, they tend to be darker in body color than their mainland forms, which allows them to absorb heat while basking in the cooler breezes of the islands.

Walls (1998) believes this form warrants valid species status based upon its insular location (Dominica), scale counts (258-273 ventrals), markings (blotches: 32-35 in trunk), and complete ring outlines with pale color. Others believe it to be a junior synonym to B. c. imperator. More research is needed to determine the true status of this animal.

This island form is known to moist forest habitats adjacent to plantations where rodents are numerous (Walls, 1998). Like other boas, young animals are more arboreal than their conspecific ground-dwelling adults, who are more sedentary and do not move significant distances.

Two pictures of the first black-bellied boa to be captured and scientifically described. Many herpetologists doubt this is a distinct subspecies.

Boa constrictor occidentalis

Known to hobbyists as the Argentine boa, this subspecies was once rare but recently has become more common in the hobby. Many breeders— professional and hobbyist— produce this subspecies. It is probably the third most common subspecies of boa in the US hobby.

Table 4: Size Records for Boa Constrictors

Subspecies or Variant	Location	Size (ft/m)	Source
Boa constrictor constrictor	Amazon Basin	15/4.6	de Vosjoli, 1990
Boa constrictor amarali	Bolivia	6.5/1.9	Barker, 1994
Boa constrictor imperator	Sonora, Mexico	9/2.7	Boger, 1945; Zweifel, 1960
Caulker Cay Boa	Caulker Cay, Belize	5/1.5	Russo, 2004
Corn Island Boa	Corn Island, Nicaragua	3.5/1.1	Russo, 2004
Crawl Key Boa	Crawl Key Island	2.3/0.7	Ronne, 1996
Hog Island Boa	Hog Island, Honduras	5/1.5	Russo, 2004
Leopard Boa	Sonora Desert, Mexico	5/1.5	Russo, 2004
Tarahumara Boa	Sierra Tarahumara, Mexico	3/0.9	Russo, 2004
Boa constrictor nebulosus	Dominica	6/1.8	Walls, 1998
Boa constrictor occidentalis	Argentina/Bolivia	12/3.7	Bertone, 2003
Boa constrictor orophias	Praslin, St. Lucia	7.5/2.3	Lazell, 1964
Boa constrictor ortonii	Peru	4/1.2	de Vosjoli, 1997
Boa constrictor sabogae	San Jose Island, Panama	3.2/0.9	Barbour, 1906

Found principally near the Andes Mountains in Argentina, Bolivia, and Paraguay, it is the darkest of the entire boa constrictor complex. Living in the cooler climates of higher elevations and temperate latitudes, its darker color allows it to soak up the much needed solar radiation. Some specimens are almost black with white splattering throughout the body; others may have a charcoal grey background, with a black and white scale pattern. Some have a pinkish cast to their coloration. Like Amaral's boa—the boa closest geographically—Argentine boas lack red saddles on the tail.

In his assessment, Dr. Thomas Barbour believed this species to be a distinct and valid subspecies of the boa constrictor complex due to its isolation from other mainland populations and subspecies of boa (Barbour, 1924). Jerry Walls (1998) has suggested that this Argentine subspecies is the most distinct of the boa constrictor complex and may merit being reclassified as a separate species, as Dr. Thomas Barbour also suggested in his assessment in 1924. The coloration, pattern, and scale counts are different than other subspecies. However, there are a number of similarities between this subspecies and *B. c. amarali*. Genetic research has indicated that *B. c. occidentalis* has only recently diverged from other boas (Rivera et al., 2005). Further research is needed to determine the status of this snake.

In Argentina's Chaco region, this subspecies is known to inhabit xeric habitats. The annual temperatures range from 64°-73°F (18°-23°C), with rainfall ranging from 12-21 inches (300-550 mm), a dry period from April to September, and a wet season from October to March. This subspecies preys on and inhabits the burrows of the viscacha (*Lagostomus maximus*), a large rodent. It lives in large communal warrens, called viscacherias, that can cover 2,000 square feet (about 610 m) of territory containing perhaps 20-30 individuals. These subterranean viscacheria entrances may be a yard (1 m) in diameter, and other animals may dwell in them, including owls and boas (Sanderson, 1972)!

Wild-caught Argentine boas are aggressive and will not hesitate to strike you, but captive born animals readily calm down and can be quite docile. However, the subspecies has a reputation among hobbyists for being a belligerent snake.

The clouded boa is only found on the Caribbean island of Dominica.

Boa constrictor orophias

Another of the island subspecies, B. c. *orophias* is found on the Caribbean island of St. Lucia, and its most common name is the St. Lucian boa. It is a rarity in the pet trade, but it is being bred by some European herpetoculturists.

There is no doubt that this subspecies is closely related to B. c. *constrictor*. Although this subspecies closely corresponds with *Boa constrictor constrictor* on Trinidad and Tobago in characteristics, it is darker in color and has more dorsal saddles (Lazell, 1964).

Walls (1998) believes this form warrants species status, and formally states his opinions for such elevation: its isolated locality (St. Lucia), scale count (ventrals 270-288, greater than other B. *constrictor* subspecies), markings, and its dark color on a pale brown body. This species often displays a unique color difference from one end of its body to the other—its anterior end versus its posterior end—and the tail end is often much darker and strikingly patterned than the head end. The tail is dark an does not have reddish saddles.

Boa constrictor orophias is known locally as Tete Chien (dog head) boa. It is known to Trinidad in the Northern Hills region, between Moruga and Point Galeota on the southern coast. This boa is often found in wet ravines and can be found as high as 1,050 feet (350 m). Specimens of this subspecies have been reported in St. Lucia and the Dominican Republic as well (Mole, 1924; Lazell, 1964). Several herpetoculturists have brought it to my attention that they have never heard of B. c. *orophias* occurring anywhere but on St. Lucia. There is certainly the possibility of misidentifications, since B. c. *constrictor* does occur on Trinidad. Additionally, the Dominican Republic is quite distant to St. Lucia, which makes one wonder how St. Lucian boas got there. This creates considerable confusion as to what the actual range of B. c. *orophias* is. Further research is needed.

This boa subspecies is a more tree-loving inhabitant; so if you keep it, include an arboreal environment for your animal, more so than for other boa constrictors. Specimens reaching 6-7 feet (1.8-2.1 m) in length have been observed in trees, so make sure your enclosures have sturdy branches for adults to climb on as well.

Endangered Argentines

This subspecies has been classified as endangered by CITES (Convention on the International Trade of Endangered Species) due to the increased loss of its natural habitat, and persecution of this species for export as a commodity in the skin-trade market (Rivera et al., 2005).

Boa constrictor ortonii

This subspecies was initially collected at Chilete, a town near Pacasmayo, Peru, 3,000 feet (914.4 m) above sea level. Professor James Orton, whose explorations of the western regions of South America were exemplary, collected this specimen. Hence, paleontologist Edward Drinker Cope (1840-1897) formally named *Boa constrictor ortonii* in his honor in 1878. It is usually called Orton's boa or the Peruvian boa by hobbyists; the latter name is confusing, because two other subspecies of boa occur in Peru. It is sometimes called the western boa. It is present but not common in the hobby.

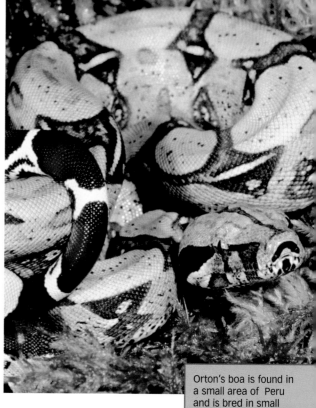

Orton's boa is found in a small area of Peru and is bred in small numbers by hobbyists.

Boa constrictor ortonii has a characteristic silvery or blue-grey background color, with crisp black markings. This subspecies has a body coloration resembling its habitat. It ranges from Perico and the upper Maranon Valley to Piura, south to Libertad within the more arid regions of northwestern Peru. *B. c. ortonii* has a high saddle count, 22-28, which is similar to that of Amaral's boa. It has 60-80 dorsal scale rows and 246-252 ventral scales.

The Andes Mountains divides Peru into principally three distinct regions: the costa, the sierra, and the montana. The costa is the desert coast with its numerous oases dispersed intermittently across it. The sierra is that region of high elevations where plateaus and mountain ridges extend far above the snow line. The montana is that region where the tropical forests lie in the deep valleys of the surrounding ridges and is connected to the Amazonian lowland east of the mountains. These divisions are mirrored by the distributions of plants and animals; usually, an organism is found in one are and not the others (Schmidt, 1943). Most of the snakes inhabiting the desert costa zone are endemic, which means they are found only in that region.

Mexican Boas

The boas found in Mexico north of the Isthmus of Tehuantepec were once considered to be a distinct subspecies, *Boa constrictor mexicana*. The boas from this area tend to be dark in color with a rather muddy pattern. Many have an iridescent sheen. However, these differences are not enough to regard Mexican boas as a separate subspecies. The boas from Mexico are all *B. c. imperator*.

Similarly, the boas found on the Tres Marias Islands off the Pacific Coast of Mexico were also considered a separate subspecies, Boa constrictor sigma. These, too, are now considered just a variant of *B. c. imperator*.

Boa constrictor sabogae

This rare boa is usually called the Taboga (or Saboga) Island boa. Sometimes, it is called the Pearl Island boa because Taboga is one of the Pearl Islands. It is a pale boa with a reduced pattern.

As part of the John E. Thayer Expedition of 1904, W.W. Brown, Jr., collected vertebrates for the Museum of Comparative Zoology, Harvard University. Among one of the specimens he collected, and forthwith Dr. Thomas Barbour described, is an insular (island) form of the boa constrictor complex (Barbour, 1906). The boa specimens Mr. Brown collected were taken from Saboga Island.

A boa from northern Mexico.

This insular (island) form has only been found on Taboga Island, in the country of Panama in 1904 (Barbour, 1906). The majority of the animals found on Taboga Island are not fundamentally different than those found on the mainland in semi-arid habitats and have little pattern on them. Some people believe this snake is different enough to warrant a subspecific status within the boa constrictor group while others do not.

Hog Island boas are a local variant of the common Central American boa.

Dwarfism Among Boas

Dwarfism among reptiles is not unique, it is merely a genetic expression of the genes and chromosomes of a particular animal. However, dwarfism appears to occur more frequently on islands where most of the wildlife there is restricted in movement (stuck on the island), has limited food resources, engages in nocturnal behavior, and has limited competition for all resources, along with the genetic expression of the animal itself. Hence, there is a propensity for dwarfism among island populations, especially among predators (Carlquist, 1965; Russo, 2004).

In the Sonora Desert, isolated habitat zones also hold the animals that live there captive within them. Some boa constrictors that have been seen there are blond, mustard, or orange in background color. It is speculated that these snakes may reach a maximum length of 6 feet (1.8 m) (Russo, 2004).

The dwarf boa constrictors described below—whether they are valid subspecies or not—make excellent apartment pets as they require less space and food than their larger counterparts. Being extremely beautiful and striking, they have become highly desirable in the pet trade today.

Hog Island Boas *Cayos de los Cochinos* translates to "Island of the Hogs," as named by the Spanish explorer Hernan Cortes (1485-1547), who reportedly raised pigs there. Hog Island has regions of lush tropical forests, which may be in jeopardy because of habitat destruction and invasive plant species (Russo, 2004). A unique form of boa constrictor occurs there, and it is currently considered a variant of *B. c. imperator*. The Hog Island boa, which tends to be smaller than its mainland Honduras counterpart, often exhibits a mutant coloration of its body with a complete lack of red pigments. However, there are populations of boas very

Table 5: Longevity Records for Boas

Subspecies	Years & Months	Location	Source
Boa constrictor constrictor	40 yrs. 3 mos.	Philadelphia Zoo	de Vosjoli, 1990
Boa constrictor amarali	15 yrs. 7 mos.	Hopewell, NY	Bowler, 1977; Carey, 2000
Boa constrictor imperator	29 yrs. 1 mo.	Philadelphia Zoo	Bowler, 1997
Boa constrictor ortonii	11 yrs. 11 mos.	Colombus Zoo	Bowler, 1977; Carey, 2000

similar in appearance to Hog Island boas found on the mainland. These boas are pale in color and often show pink, peach, and tan colors. The tail is never reddish but instead is chocolate brown, burnt orange, or similarly colored. Many keepers have reported that these boas change color with time of day, season, and exposure to light.

With continued forest destruction on the islands and the massive export of thousands of boas from 1979 to 1986, this subspecies population may be threatened by extinction on the islands. Two herpetological surveys of Hog Island report that by 1993 no Hog Island boas were found there (Russo, 2004). Hence, as Jerry Walls has stated, this island morph may already be extinct in the wild and known only in the pet trade today (Walls, 1998).

These boas have become fairly common in the pet trade, although they are rarely seen in pet stores. Many breeders produce this variety, and they are often sold at herp expos. They remain more expensive than Central American boas.

Caulker Cay Boas Another insular form, the Caulker boa derives from Caulker Cay, a small island 19 miles from Belize. Like the Hog Island form, it is also small, reaching a maximum length of 5 feet (1.5 m). These boas are lean animals, with adult bodies the diameter of a broom handle. The neonates are smaller than those of most other subspecies and must be fed small prey.

They are gray to grayish brown with very dark dorsal saddles. They have 22-24 dorsal saddles. These boas lack red pigment (anerythristic); the belly is white with speckled grey and black. They are arboreal, seeking out birds as prey, as they are probably the most abundant food resource on the island. Predators include crabs and man. Although Caulker boas start out aggressive, they do calm down. Also, being dwarf forms, they take up little space in your home (Russo, 2004).

Corn Island Boas Off the shore of Nicaragua, 50 miles east, is Islas del Maize, or Corn Island. In 1995, two farmed litters of 21 neonate boas of this insular form were imported into the United States, hence they are rarely encountered in pet collections anywhere (Russo, 2004). Since 1995, Islas del Maize has become a protected reserve, so it is unlikely that any additional individual will be forthcoming anytime soon.

Corn Island boas have a background color of olive green to green and tan; this is the only form that exhibits green body coloration. It has approximately 23 dorsal saddles. The ventral is rose pink in juveniles and later fades to white or cloudy green in adults. Like the Hog Island boas, these boas show great changes in color. These are muscular, slender snakes.

Copulation takes places in a manner that other arboreal snakes exhibit—in a knotted ball. Corn Island boas, sexually mature at 3 years of age and at a length of 42 inches (total length), are able to rear litters of 14 babies. Unlike the Caulker Cay forms, this island form is docile (Russo, 2004).

Tarahumara Desert Boas The Sonora Desert is a vast, dry, hot, but most beautiful place to visit. In this desert, there are small oases or forested plateaus. Although usually regarded as a hot place, the desert can also be frigidly cold, especially at night and more so at higher elevations. These oasis plateaus are analogous to islands in the Pacific and Caribbean as they are restricted environments unto themselves, restricted by a hot or cold sea of sand that creates a barrier surrounding them.

The red-tailed boas found on Corn Island tend to stay smaller than typical boas and are often greenish in color, although this Corn Island boa is not.

Living on these desert plateaus is the Tarahumara Desert boa, which ranges throughout the northern Mexican states of Chihuahua and Sonora among the Sierra Tarahumara Mountains. It is found at high elevations of 4,000 feet (1.2 km) among forested plateaus with deeply eroded riparian canyons or ravines (Russo, 2004). It is currently considered a variant of B. c. *imperator*.

This plateau form is beige to white in background color, with distinct black blotches. Younger specimens have a pink coloration between the saddle patches. In adult Tarahumara boas, the tail turns from rust to a jet-black color, and the overall body color darkens somewhat. They have a high dorsal saddle count from 26 to 29. Dark colors absorb more heat than lighter colors, so this darker body coloration is probably an adaptation to heat collecting and habitat surroundings (Russo, 2004).

Tarahumara boas are loud hissers and aggressive, but readily calm down in captivity. With their diminutive size and docility in captivity, this rare boa makes an ideal cohabitant in your home.

Leopard Boas Like the Tarahumara boa, this little known morph is indigenous to the Sonora Desert (Russo, 2004). Herpetoculturist Hans Winner first bred it in Germany. He showed that this pattern morph is an inheritable anomaly, a recessive trait of line breeding the siblings back to their parents (inbreeding).

This pattern morph has dorsal blotches that are broken up into stripes that fade down its marbled sides. The tail has blotches of red that become darker with age. Some individuals have gold-colored heads, while others have reddish chins. In some specimens, the faces resemble a leopard's, hence their common name. Some forms are completely striped, which is an aberrant but striking pattern for a boa constrictor (Russo, 2004).

Senses

Red-tailed boas have more or less the same senses as mammals, although some are more highly developed than in mammals and some are less so. In addition to the five senses we are most familiar with, boas can detect the heat given off by prey.

The boas found in the Sonoran Desert have evolved their dwarfed size probably as an adaptation to the limited resources in their habitat.

Vision

Snakes have unblinking eyelids. The snake has lost most of the parts of its eye that other reptiles, birds, and mammals still retain, probably as an adaptation to an underground and crepuscular lifestyle. In vertebrates other than snakes, there are chiefly two kinds of cell types within the eye's retina: rods and cones. Rods are dim-light receptors, whereas cones are bright-light receptors that can detect color. Boas and pythons have both rods and cones within their retinas, but some groups of snake have only cones (e.g., the colubrids).

The iris of the eye controls the size of the pupil, and by opening and/or closing, it permits light to be received by the eye; this control of light into the eye is a key component to sight in vertebrates. An animal that has a round pupil cannot close off the pupil to keep all light out of the eye; but an eye that is round when expanded but closes to a slit like a cat's pupil can shut out the light more effectively. Boas have this ocular arrangement.

Animals with a high number of cones see color, so it is thought that snakes can see color, which enables them to see shadows and shades of an animal's pattern as it stealthily moves through the forest at night; of course nocturnal predators prey on many animals that are themselves nocturnal and also have excellent night vision.

During shedding, the clear protective scale covering the eye is also replaced; the old "spectacles" are discarded with the rest of the sloughed skin shed. If the spectacle fails to shed off with the sloughed skin, it can cause irreparable damage to the eyes, eventually causing blindness if not corrected—see Chapter 6 for more on this topic.

Smell

The tongue is probably the most important sense organ for a snake, boas included. Most vertebrates smell using their noses, or nasal organs. The snake uses its nose and tongue to receive airborne scents. Boas have a powerful sense of smell. You may notice this yourself; observe how active your boa becomes when you thaw out a frozen mouse on the counter. Even before you bring the food into the boa's room, it may be moving actively about the cage flicking its tongue rapidly.

For the snake, the tongue is an organ of both taste and touch that transmits stimuli to another organ only snakes and lizards have, the Jacobson's organ. It provides some lizards and most snakes with reception that enables them to detect chemical stimuli indicative of prey, predators, or conspecifics. After the forked tongue receives these chemical stimuli, it withdraws back into the mouth. The tines, or points of the forked tongue, then transmit the chemicals and pheromones to the Jacobson's organ, which lies above the palate and behind the nostrils in the head, anterior to the eyes. It then processes and transmits the information to the brain for a proper action and/or reaction response (Young, 1990).

Chemoreception aids a snake in using a chemical trail to track down prey in the black of night, when their nocturnal eyesight does aid them, but in some scenarios is not as proficient as chemoreception. It also allows them to follow prey back to a burrow, detect the trails used habitually by prey species, and find mates.

Touch

Touch is important to snakes and other animals that lack limbs. This sense is fairly well developed in snakes, but has been little tested. The snake appears to have an acute perception of vibration.

Hearing

The snake lacks an external ear tympanum (eardrum), tympanic cavity, or eustachian tube, but it does have one bone of the ear. This bone connects to the hinge of the lower jaw (quadrate) and transmits vibrations from the hinge (quadrate) to the head. Snakes may not hear prey or predators approach, but they can most likely feel their vibrations long before they have visual acuity of them (Pope, 1961).

Thermal Detection

Red-tailed boas have excellent senses of smell and taste and good vision.

Some species of snake have pits in their faces that enable them to detect the heat given off by mammalian and avian prey. While some other members of the boa family have these pits, red-tailed boas and anacondas do not. Nevertheless, they can detect radiant heat, but, of course, not as well as those snake species with labial heat-detecting pits (Pope, 1961).

Behavior

The two basic modes of behavior in the life of most reptiles are activity and inactivity, or sleep. Boa constrictors spend roughly, but not absolutely, 12 hours being active and 12 hours at rest or asleep. But boa constrictors are nocturnal, active during the night seeking out prey at ambush sites and looking for shelter after ingesting a meal. They rest during the day in a burrow, in a low-light intensity region where they are safe from predators and conspecifics (other boas).

Although you can alter the feeding schedule of your boa, if the animal is nocturnal and feeds during the night, it's best to make its life more comfortable by feeding it during the early evening, which will allow it to act as it would in its natural habitat. You will see more behaviors exhibited, and the overall health of the animal can be enhanced by these small incentives; this is commonly done with animals in the care of many zoos.

Locomotion

Boa constrictors do not move very fast, although they can be agile in their maneuvers. In field studies, they do not venture far from any given area. Not appearing to be great travelers, they are more like wanderers within a select range, patrolling their local regions intimately in every nook, cranny, tree, and bush for food, shelter, and thermoregulation.

Swimming and Climbing

Snakes are agile, patient predators, and boa constrictors are no different. They can swim, although they seldom do. They will drink freely from a water basin in captivity and may soak when the climate is uncomfortably high for them, as most reptiles and other animals do to cool off when it is too hot. However, if a reptile should be in a pool of water when the temperature drops, it may become too cooled down, and this can have a deleterious effect on it; so provide the boa with sufficient water to drink, but not enough to become entirely submerged and over-cooled.

Boa constrictors are also apt climbers and can appear to climb vertical walls if they desire. They are good tree climbers, especially the younger individuals—a 9-foot (2.7 m) adult could climb a tree, but it would be cumbersome for it to do so. They are three-dimensional predators over land, in water, and in the trees, which leaves few prey animals they cannot reach!

Denning

Aggregation among snakes is not uncommon, even among the largest snakes. Large or small, aggregations usually consist of a large female with several subordinate-sized males and may be a prelude to mating behavior (Pope, 1961; Myres, 1968). Boa constrictors use the burrows of medium sized mammals as a retreat.

Thermal aggregation (huddling together to stay warm) has been noted in wild boa constrictors (Lazell, 1964; Myers, 1968; Greene, 1983). Denning often occurs in places where there is a lack of suitable dens. It is not a behavior unique to any subspecies or the ecology of the boa in particular, but is moreso an artifact of den scarcity.

Boas sometimes can be observed basking together to reduce heat loss. This is known as aggregative behavior, which is seen more frequently with venomous snakes such as rattlesnakes (*Crotalus sp.*) throughout North, Central, and South America.

Defensive Behavior

Boa constrictors vary in temperament; some are docile when freely handled in the wild, while others can be extremely defensive. As a rule of thumb, those individuals found in South America tend to be mild-mannered in disposition, while those individuals found in Central America tend to have a nasty disposition. An exception to this may be the Argentine boa, which has a reputation for defensive behavior.

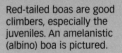

Red-tailed boas are good climbers, especially the juveniles. An amelanistic (albino) boa is pictured.

The predominant defensive behavior of the boa constrictor is the hiss. Some animals hiss with their mouths slightly opened, heads held up at a 45° angle, bodies in an S-shaped ready-to-strike posture. As boas have long, recurved teeth, a bite from even a subadult can prove nasty in its laceration. The next defensive behavior often observed is the strike, which can also result in a nasty wound. Fortunately, the strike distance of the boa constrictor is short, and with repeated strikes, the boa can easily become tired. Its third defense behavior

Prey

In the wild, several of the animals that boa constrictors prey upon are herbivorous and frugivorous and are often found among fruit-bearing trees. They include agoutis, coatimundis, high woods dogs (a badger relative), mongoose, opossums of various species, and prehensile-tailed porcupine (*Coendou rothchildi*). There are many rats and other rodents native to the boa's habitat. This is consistent with the boa constrictor's habitat preferences, and, as such, it seems logical that it would dwell where the food it prefers to consume would be more available and abundant.

is the retreat. If one survives a possibly lethal entanglement with a nemesis today, one can fight another day; and that is exactly the tactic the boa will use when all other deterrents fail.

Feeding

Among the world's largest snakes, the boa constrictor is roughly fifth in total possible size attainment. In South America, it is outsized only by its aquatic counterpart, the anaconda (*Eunectes murinus*) and possibly by the yellow anaconda (*E. notaeus*). Being nocturnal hunters, boas are somewhat inactive during daylight hours.

Luring and Stalking Prey

In nature, food is not always readily available, so the boa constrictor must seek it out. Generally being an ambush predator, it is easier for a victim to come to it, rather than having to go to its victim; but the boa constrictor apparently uses both strategies.

A snake recognizes prey by using visual, thermal, and chemical cues. Being such visual predators, movement first attracts the attention of the boa. Stalking the prey, it moves very slowly, with its head up and parallel to the ground, undulating in a forward motion. As it slithers along, it ever so slightly moves its head laterally from left to right as it seeks out or acquires initial sight of its prey. This lateral side-to-side motion is how the snake determines its distance from the food item. Making the necessary calculations, it then proceeds with a strike, finally grasping and consuming it.

Attacking Prey The tongue is the boa constrictor's primary sense organ, enabling it to perceive prey at a distance of 20 inches (50 cm) or so. While hunting, its visual acuity will

The camouflaging pattern of the red-tailed boa allows it to remain unnoticed by prey until it is too late.

aid it in recognizing a prey item's movements, thus activating a seizing reflex. The strike of a boa constrictor is exceedingly fast. The boa uses its formidable recurved teeth to prevent its prey from escaping its grasp. Then, it uses its muscular body to lift it off the ground, wrap its smooth, scaled body around it, and suffocates it with its constricting "coil of death" (Pope, 1961; Greene, 1978). Note that the boa does not crush its prey. It closes the coils tighter to prevent the prey from breathing. Constriction ceases when the prey stops moving. Following the prey's immobility, the snake locates its head and begins to swallow it.

Swallowing Prey Following the death of prey by constriction, the snake begins to consume it, head first, regardless of how small or large it may be. In the process of swallowing a prey item of manageable size, ingestion, which is usually a slow process, can take perhaps 15 minutes, and longer with larger meals. The teeth hold the prey, while the mouth "snake-walks" over the prey, moving it into the esophagus and throat regions to the stomach. After ingesting a meal, the boa will seek out a hiding place and stay there until it digests the meal.

Pet Considerations

Having covered the basic natural history of these magnificent animals, we move on to all of the information necessary to consider purchasing one of your own. The first and most important thing to remember when contemplating owning any subspecies of red-tailed boa is to do plenty of research. Do not be afraid to ask the breeder or reptile store employee any questions that you may have about the animal and its care. Keep in mind that opinions and experiences vary, so look into different sources and see what the general consensus is concerning your inquiry.

If you buy a boa, you will soon be living with a very large snake. Be prepared.

As a responsible pet owner, you must commit to regularly feeding your pet as well as regularly cleaning and maintaining a terrarium for an animal that cannot take care of itself. Because the red-tailed boa can attain considerable size, common sense and assistance are required. Always remember that even a captive-bred "pet" boa is still a wild animal and must be handled with the utmost respect. Expect to experience aggression from even the most seemingly tame snake, and you will not be caught off guard.

Being a reptile keeper, you must also expose yourself to some graphic instances: observing the constriction of live prey, removing foul smelling feces or regurgitated, partially digested rodents, and perhaps even being bitten (accidentally, in most cases) by your snake. So, being responsible for them is not merely just feeding and cleaning up after them—you are more or less a surrogate parent, and should you decide to keep a red-tailed boa in your home, you must accept this role.

Important Questions

Here are some questions to ask yourself when deciding on purchasing a boa.

Why do I want a snake?

If you want a boa because you think it would be a good way to look macho, attract attention to yourself, intimidate people, or other selfish reasons, then you are clearly not going to be a responsible pet owner. Snakes should not be something to show off. It is a stressful experience for the animal to be taken out in public. If you want a snake because you are fascinated by them and want to learn more from them, then you are on the right track.

Kids and Boas

Many times, it is one of the children in a family who really wants a boa. Children are often fascinated by snakes, and some will persistently ask if they can have a boa. Due to their eventual size, a red-tailed boa is not the best pet for a child. A smaller snake, like a corn snake or ball python, is a better option. A red-tailed boa can be kept in the same house as a child, as long as an adult is responsible for the care of the snake and the child is never allowed to handle it without an adult present.

Am I comfortable with handling a potentially aggressive snake and willing to risk the dangers associated with owning a large snake?

Though boas can seem to become tame after some regular handling, you should never assume that your snake is never going to bite. Baby boas are naturally defensive until they become acclimated to handling, and adult boas can be dangerous due to the size of their teeth, and their strong bodies have the potential of choking an adult.

Is my family okay with snakes, as well as keeping rodents in our freezer?

Make sure your family is comfortable with the idea of your new pet before you get it. It is best to educate them in the proper methods of handling and care so they can be an extra set of eyes looking out for its well-being when you aren't around. Some people are disgusted at the thought of rodents in their freezer with their food, so make sure they are okay with this. Having a small "rodents only" freezer may go a long way to ensuring your domestic tranquility.

Can my kids handle snakes?

Children are often mystified by snakes if they haven't been around them before. Encourage their interest in reptiles, but make sure they understand the dangers associated with handling, salmonella risks, etc. Kids should always be closely supervised when handling any reptile and should never be allowed to handle large, potentially dangerous adult boas. Boas are not recommended as a first pet snake for kids. There are plenty of smaller, relatively docile species that make better first pets.

Is there a veterinarian in my area that is experienced with reptile medicine?

Before purchasing a reptile, you must make sure you know of a veterinarian in your area who is experienced with the specialized medical care required for reptiles. Many health

Always supervise children when they are handling a boa or any other snake.

problems can arise shortly after purchasing your snake, so it is best to know where to take it for care in an emergency.

Am I able to afford all the supplies and food that my boa will require?

Though keeping snakes isn't as expensive as some pets, the supplies and food required does cost more than one would initially think. Research the supplies you will need before purchasing your snake, and determine how much everything will cost and make sure you can afford it. Remember that vet visits can be expensive as well. Do not cut corners simply because you can't afford all the necessary supplies. If the supplies cost too much, you are not ready to own a snake at this time.

Will I be able to take care of my boa when it reaches adult size?

Far too many people end up getting rid of their snake when it reaches its large adult size. Often, they weren't prepared for the cost of feeding a large snake, as well as the amount of space it takes up, added dangers, etc. It is also more difficult than one would think to sell or even give away a large boa. Many people are under the impression that zoos will accept them, but generally they won't. Unfortunately, many irresponsible owners end up releasing their large boa as a last resort, which either results in the snake dying of cold or, in warm areas, it can result in established breeding populations that threaten native animals, as has already happened in south Florida.

Are there restrictions in my area prohibiting the ownership of boas?

Due mainly to misconceptions among the general public and the actions of irresponsible reptile keepers, laws are often introduced banning or restricting the keeping of large, potentially dangerous reptiles in certain areas. Some areas may require licenses to own boas. It is important to check for any restrictions in your area. Your local pet store should be able to help you with this information. Some landlords and homeowner's associations may frown upon the keeping of reptiles as well.

Before You Bring One Home

Before purchasing any reptile, you should make sure to have a cage with all the necessary furnishings set up in advance. In this way, you can get the cage set up, temperatures adjusted, and make sure all equipment is working properly, which will allow for a less stressful acclimation period for your new snake. Fortunately, most supplies can be purchased at any pet store that offers reptiles. You should also make sure you have a reliable source of rodents. Once you have set up your cage and have a reliable source of food items, you can begin looking for your new pet.

Finding a Healthy Red-Tailed Boa

Advances in modern husbandry and a better understanding of boas have led to the availability of reasonably priced captive-bred animals of every size and color pattern imaginable. However, the task of finding a healthy and ideal pet boa can require some careful research and planning.

Three Options

Boas offered for sale are either captive bred, imports, or "farm raised." Captive-bred snakes are far more desirable than the other types. These are the offspring of established captive snakes that are likely to have the fewest problems adapting to a caged lifestyle and will be among the healthiest. Buying captive-bred snakes also helps conserve wild populations, reducing the demand for parasite-infested imports that don't do as well in captivity.

Salmonella Risks

As with all reptiles, there is the possibility of contracting a *Salmonella* bacterial infection (salmonellosis) from red-tailed boas. This can result in severe gastric distress and diarrhea and—in rare cases—can be fatal. You should always wash your hands before and after handling any reptile, your boa included. Although there is some risk of getting salmonellosis from your snake and you should take precautions against contracting it, remember to put the risk in perspective. There is probably more risk of getting salmonellosis from eating undercooked chicken and eggs than there is from handling your boa.

Questions to Ask Before Purchasing a Boa

When asking about a company or breeder:
- How long have you been in business?
- How long have you kept red-tailed boas?
- Where do the boas in question originate from?
- Do you sterilize cages and equipment between animals?

When purchasing a juvenile:
- Can I see the parents (or pictures of them)?
- How old was the mother?
- When was this animal born?
- Has it shed? When was the last time it shed?
- Has it eaten? How often is it fed, and what is it being fed?
- May I see it eat? Or, may I return to see it eat?
- May I compare it to its siblings?

Farm-raised boas are the offspring of wild-collected gravid (pregnant with eggs) females temporarily held in captivity in their native homeland until they give birth to their babies. The juveniles are then shipped around the world to eventually enter the pet trade. Often, they are shipped very shortly after birth to an importer, who then may immediately ship them to their customers, at which point they finally get their first drink of water. Since holding conditions may not be clean in their country of origin, the possibility of contracting parasites is high, and newborn, recently imported boas sometimes have mites or ticks on them, as well as internal parasites.

Imported wild-caught boas are usually of larger size and are collected directly from the wild and exported to other countries. Imports often have trouble adjusting to captive life, are aggressive, and present many parasite problems. A certain percentage does not survive the transition to captivity, and wild populations are impacted from continued collecting. With the increasing availability of captive-born boas, there is no need to purchase wild-caught snakes for pets.

Sources of Boas

For many, the internet is the first and easiest resource to explore. This can be good or bad, depending on the questions you ask and the information you acquire. Many breeders have websites offering their current inventory, and some even have pictures of individual snakes allowing the buyer to choose the one he likes. There are many websites created by serious boa hobbyists as well, and searching these sites will often provide good leads on reputable online sources for quality animals.

Do not make hasty purchases; always take the time to make sure the company, breeder, or store you buy from is experienced and knowledgeable, believes in their animals, and is willing to help you properly obtain your new boa. Be careful—keep in mind that whatever box lands on your front porch, its contents will end up yours, dead or alive, with few refunds available.

A pet store that specializes in reptiles is probably the best bet for finding your first boa. There is no comparison to being able to personally inspect potential purchases. When you walk through a store, take notice of the condition of the animals and how they are kept. If they appear healthy, the enclosures are clean and free of obvious external parasites, and the staff seems knowledgeable, you are ready to start asking questions. Be wary of sales people who are reluctant or unable to provide answers to any inquiries you may have. It is in the best interest of a reputable breeder or store to provide you with a healthy animal.

Aside from pet stores, there are many commercial and private reptile breeders that provide quality animals. Some specialize in boas, and it is from these breeders that one can choose from a wider variety of colors and ages of snakes. Some breeders will be selling fresh-born boas to avoid having to feed and take care of them, while other breeders prefer to "head-start" their babies, keeping them for several weeks before offering them for sale. This ensures that their animals are healthy and feeding, which is of course preferable to purchasing a newborn boa.

The best red-tailed boa to purchase is a well-started, captive-bred baby.

Another source for healthy boas is one of the many reptile shows held at least annually in larger cities. Often, breeders will have a wide selection you may choose from and will usually be very willing to share helpful advice. It is a convenient way to shop around with various vendors at the same time.

Health Inspection

When you have found a pet shop or breeder that sells red-tailed boas, look at the snakes carefully. Are they colorful or dull? Is the animal skinny or fat? Is it a male or a female? Being prepared with some insights and knowledge of the animal before you walk in the door will help to ensure that the boa you bring home will be a healthy new pet.

Warning Signs

Below is a list of signs you should look out for when inspecting a boa for purchase. If you notice any of these signs, you should select a different one.

- boa has any lumps, kinks, or swollen areas
- boa has ticks or mites (small crawling spots) on body or in cage
- boa is limp or has no muscle tone
- bubbling or foaming in the nostrils
- mouth has cheesy matter inside
- vent has crusted feces or other material around it

When you see an animal that catches your eye, ask the clerk to allow you to have a closer look at it outside of the terrarium. See if you can handle it. If so, hold the snake gently, allowing it to freely crawl through your arms. If the animal is limp and non-muscular, pass the snake back to the clerk and ask to see another one. Although not always fun, a healthy snake may have a nasty, agitated disposition. However, if it is too aggressive for you, seek out another more docile candidate. Any animal that you are apprehensive about handling should cause you to reconsider your choice of pet. Remember, a snake is a wild animal, and both you and the boa have to establish a relationship before you feel comfortable living with each other. It is not wise to purchase a snake to impress your friends—it won't be very impressive if you are too scared to handle it!

During the inspection process, check the animal carefully. A healthy snake should have clear eyes with no discharge, and the inside of the mouth should be clean with no "cheesy'" material present around the gums or inside the oral cavity (a sign of stomatitis, or mouth rot). Look the animal over for kinks, bumps, muscle irregularities, cuts, abrasions, burns, scars, etc. Also check the nostrils and cloaca region (the vent located at the base of the tail) for ticks and inspect the skin folds for mites. Listen closely for wheezing or whistling noises as the snake breathes, but do not confuse this with the hissing noise of a defensive snake. If you have examined the snake for all of these conditions, and you like what you find, you are ready to purchase the snake.

If you order your boa from a distant source, make sure the seller is knowledgeable with shipping live reptiles properly. Shipping during the winter and summer months is tricky, as the package containing the reptiles may be exposed to a variety of temperature extremes that can be fatal. Some breeders use heat packs and cold packs during these times of the year, but even these can cause harm if not used properly. Baby boas are normally shipped in plastic deli cups with ventilation holes punched in the sides, and a slightly damp paper towel lining the bottom of the cup for humidity. Larger boas are often shipped in pillowcases or other suitable sized cloth bags. These are packed in cardboard boxes insulated with foam inserts. Reptiles should only be shipped for overnight delivery and should never be in transit for longer than 24 hours. Always be available to receive the package and unpack the animal immediately upon arrival.

Before you purchase a boa, look it over carefully for any signs of ill health. Never purchase a sickly boa.

Acclimation and Quarantine

When bringing home a newly purchased boa, it is best to avoid handling it for several days so it doesn't have to undergo additional stress. This allows the snake to get used to its new environment. Make sure to provide appropriate hiding places to make it feel more secure.

If the snake was shipped to you, it has just gone through a very stressful experience. After a long time in transit, the boa will be thirsty, and a water bowl must be available. Don't try to feed it yet, as it will most likely refuse food until it settles in.

In general, red-tailed boas should be kept solitary, except when they are breeding. If you already own other reptiles, newly purchased animals should always be placed in quarantine away from the rest of the collection to be sure they are free from any communicable health problems. Most serious issues should make themselves apparent within the first few months or so, at which time a visit to the vet may be in order. The health of any new animal should be closely monitored during this time. The snake should be placed into isolation for at least three months.

During quarantine, place the new animal in its own terrarium and check on it periodically while it becomes accustomed to its new home. The quarantine area should be similar to the permanent enclosure, with attention paid to appropriate temperature, humidity, and proper hygienic protocol. Using newspaper as a substrate in your quarantine tank also allows you to check the feces for any abnormalities. Be sure to wash your hands before and after you enter the enclosure. Also, have a set of supplies (cleaning supplies, hide boxes, etc.) that are designated only for your snake in quarantine. If any problem manifests while your new pet is in quarantine, seek veterinary attention immediately.

Chapter 3

Housing and Handling

Your newly purchased boa is a wild animal and will be relying solely on you to provide all of the proper conditions it needs to live a long, healthy life. Knowing the natural history of the species you choose is the best place to start. But it isn't enough to help you successfully keep boas in captivity if you don't know how to translate useful information into usable husbandry practice. Wild boas adapt to conditions available to them in their natural habitats to achieve their goals—be it hunting for food, reproducing, or for finding shelter from the elements. It is up to you to do your best to replicate these conditions in order to allow your boa to establish and maintain its health.

Proper housing is crucial to the health of your red-tailed boa.

Boas use a variety of natural features for different purposes. They use dens, burrows, tree hollows, rock crevices, and even human settlements to maintain an acceptable body temperature, to protect against predators, and to find receptive mating partners. They utilize game trails and other animal dens for hunting and ambush. At first glance, all of these requirements may seem impossible to achieve in captivity, but all of the essential elements are relatively easy to provide.

Types of Cages

Proper housing and good captive husbandry are crucial to providing a quality life for your snake. As mentioned earlier, boa constrictors in captivity should be housed separately, except during breeding season when the male must be introduced to the female. In choosing an enclosure, be aware that different housing scenarios are required for each life stage. Juveniles, subadults, and adults will require a slightly different approach when it comes to providing proper temperature, humidity, and amount of space.

Cage Security

Snakes are notorious escape artists, and red-tailed boas are no exception. Remember that boas are powerful animals and can push open cage doors and screen tops with ease. To prevent the loss of your pet, your cage should have some form of lock. The doors must be sturdily constructed. Inspect your cage periodically for any weak points—loose door hinges, corroded ventilation screens, etc.—and repair them immediately. It is easier to prevent an escape than it is to find an escaped boa.

For juveniles, some keepers recommend starting with a 10 gallon (37.9 l) aquarium, but these and other open-topped enclosures are not recommended for boas. Screened tops simply allow all of the essential heat and humidity to escape. Similarly, humidity—another necessary component of proper care—is rapidly lost in an open-top enclosure. Larger aquariums are designed more for fish than for reptiles, and the floor area is often long and narrow and doesn't allow the snake to stretch out in more than one direction. If you must use an aquarium for housing your juvenile, use a large water bowl to increase the humidity in the cage, and mist the cage at least two times per day with a spray bottle.

Designing an enclosure and building it yourself, or having someone build it for you, will give you the best results. Custom-made wooden cages with glass fronts can be very attractive and are recommended. The wood and corners must be sealed to prevent humidity, feces, etc. from absorbing into the wood, which would otherwise rot or warp the cage. Some keepers build their cages out of melamine or sheets of PVC, which is much easier to clean. Make sure the glass is securely fixed into place and is thick enough that a strong adult boa cannot push against it and break it. Cages with sliding glass panes that serve as doors into the cage must be secured, as large snakes have been known to inadvertently slide them open when simply rubbing their body against them. When designing your enclosure, be sure to measure all doorways in your home through which it will have to pass.

There are several companies that make glass-fronted, molded plastic or fiberglass cages. These often have designated areas for heat lamps, heat tape, or other furnishings and are an excellent choice for those who do not want to construct their own cage.

Other companies manufacture rack systems in which molded plastic tubs suitable for juvenile to subadult boas slide into a vertically standing rack holding several cages. Though space-efficient for housing multiple snakes, these are usually practical for those who are seriously breeding snakes, as they do not offer any view of the snake through the opaque tub.

Temperature and Heating

Boa constrictors are secretive animals, yet they are able to maintain preferred body temperatures without basking outright, as many lizards and other snakes must do. Natural temperature ranges for most boas fluctuate little. This species can tolerate a range from 78.8-93.2°F (26-34°C), with an average temperature preference of approximately 86°F (30°C), so they tend to thermoregulate in an area where this ambient temperature range is provided (Brattstrom, 1965).

Whether you are housing a juvenile boa for the first time or setting up a larger enclosure for your rapidly growing subadult, temperature and humidity should be your first consideration. An ambient temperature around 85°F (29.4°C)is a good start.

Regardless of the size or style of the enclosure you decide on, you will have to purchase an appropriate heat source. Many enclosure manufacturers build their cages to accept certain types of heating sources, and it may be best to start with their recommendations. You can always revise your heating sources to suit your snake's needs better as you gain more experience and information to make modifications as needed.

Thermal Gradient

In determining the best heating methods to suit your snake's needs, you need to understand the importance of a thermal, or temperature, gradient. This means that your boa should not be forced to live in a cage that is entirely one temperature. Your boa should be able to decide for itself at which temperature it wants to be. It should have a spot warmer than the ambient room temperature on one end of the cage, which will create a cooler spot (equal to or slightly above the ambient room temperature) on the opposite side of the cage. This way, if the snake wants to get warmer, it will choose a spot closer to the heat source, and if it wants to be cooler, it will distance itself from the heat source. A good maximum temperature to strive for in the hot end of the cage would be in the mid- to upper 90°F range (36°-37°C), while the cool end would be in the low 80s (26.7°-28.3°C), creating an area in the middle of the cage ranging in the mid- to upper 80s (29-31.1°C), depending on the distance away from the heat source.

Ambient room temperature needs to be considered, especially for large cages. You do not want the cool end of the cage to be too cold, and

No Heat Rocks!

Some pet stores still carry and recommend heat rocks. These are fake rocks with a built-in heating element, sometimes called hot rocks and sizzle stones. They do not have a means of controlling the temperature and do not create a heat gradient. The snake is forced to either cook itself on the rock or be too cold. Therefore, heat rocks are strongly discouraged.

therefore supplemental room heating may be required in the wintertime. You obviously don't want the room to get too hot as well, as this will interfere with providing a good temperature gradient. Air conditioning may be necessary in areas that get too hot, but monitor the temperatures to make sure the living conditions don't get too cold. Most keepers allow nighttime temperatures to drop about 78°F (25.6°C). This is understandable because temperatures drop naturally at night.

A good thermometer is indispensable in making sure you are providing a good temperature gradient and to make sure all heating equipment is adjusted to the proper temperature. Infrared temperature guns are a worthy investment for any reptile keeper. These handheld devices will read an accurate temperature on the surface it is pointed at, and some models allow you to get minimum and maximum temperature readings from an area scanned with the gun, valuable in creating a temperature gradient. Make it a point to check that your heat source is functioning properly on a daily basis so your pet isn't exposed to hazardous temperature extremes.

Incandescent light bulbs are among the best heat sources available. They provide heat from above (like the sun), will readily warm the right basking spot or hide, and easily allow you to tell if they are functioning properly or not. They also double as illumination so you

Dehydration

Loss of water, or dehydration, is dangerous for reptiles, as well as other vertebrates. For humans, a 20 percent loss in water per body weight causes death; for a rat or mouse, a 33 percent water loss per body weight equates death; for some snakes, only a 9.1 percent water loss per body weight may bring death. (Pope, 1961). This highlights the importance of proper humidity and clean drinking water.

can see your pet. A combination of smaller wattage bulbs is superior to one high wattage bulb, which may create a "hot spot" and thermal burns if your animal gets too close to it. Many manufacturers sell "light cages" that keep your snake from actually touching the lights. These work great, and their use is encouraged. Incandescent lights used as a heat source can be dangerous in smaller cages used for juveniles, as the heat can build up to a point where it is too hot, and there isn't a cool spot for the snake to retire to if it needs to.

Heat tape and heat pads can also be a good way to provide the appropriate temperatures and can be a good second choice that will not emit light. Heat tapes are better than heat pads for smaller cages as they do not heat up a large area. Heat tapes are best run under one end of the cage to create the necessary thermal gradient. Heat pads are better for larger cages as they heat a larger area needed by larger snakes. Some models come with a built-in temperature control, and others do not, but there are heating controls on the market specifically made for reptile keepers that allow you to set the desired temperature, and some even allow for a nighttime temperature drop.

Humidity

If the humidity level in the cage is not adequate, your snake may experience shedding problems, which if not caught in time could lead to severe problems and even death. Dehydration can also result from low levels of humidity. Juvenile boas are particularly dependent on high levels of humidity to help with their frequent shedding. Adults are more tolerant of drier conditions. Purchasing a hygrometer is recommended, especially in exceptionally dry regions.

One keeper recommends maintaining humidity levels around 80-95 percent for newborn neonate boa constrictors and maintaining them at a 40-60 percent humidity level following their first skin shed, or ecdysis (Divers, 1993). If the relative humidity in the cage is falling below this level, more frequent misting of the sides of the cage with a spray bottle

Boas require 40-60 percent relative humidity for optimum hydration.

is recommended. In smaller cages, a larger water bowl can often help maintain high humidity. In extremely dry regions, a humidifier may be a wise investment. With this equipment, the room can be kept at the proper humidity, reducing the need to regularly mist the enclosure.

Water

Clean water must be provided at all times. The water bowl should be checked daily and replaced with clean water whenever necessary. For smaller boas, try to use a water dish in which the snake can soak should it choose to do so. Often, snakes may want to soak prior to shedding.

Water quality should be of concern. City water often has chlorine and possibly other chemicals in it. Though some breeders use city water without apparent problems, others prefer to use water from cleaner sources. Well water in certain areas may have high amounts of minerals that may not be good for your snake. If you are unsure about the quality of your water, it might be best to use bottled water from a reliable source. If the water is of a quality that you don't want to drink, do not give it to your pets.

Problem Substrates

Stay away from substrates made of cedar. Though cedar chips are sold for use as a substrate for small mammals, the fragrant phenols in cedar wood are harmful to reptiles and should never be used. Similarly, do not use eucalyptus mulch.

Substrates

In reptile husbandry, substrate is the type of bedding or floor covering used inside the enclosure. There are many different choices for substrate; the type and style of your enclosure will dictate which one works best for you. Some types will work better or worse in different enclosures and at different times in your boa's life cycle. What you are looking for is a ground cover that holds humidity, provides security, is easy to clean, is inexpensive to replace when necessary, and is aesthetically pleasing—in that order.

Wood and Paper Products

Starting juveniles on newspaper, paper towel, or construction paper can be a good initial choice; paper is inexpensive or free, and feces will be easy to spot and clean up in a snap. The down side to paper is its inability to hold moisture and its unappealing appearance. It also gets moved around by the snake if not secured in some way. Keeping boas of all sizes on newspaper or corrugated packing paper is suitable; most major breeders use this exclusively.

There are several commercially available substrates that hold humidity better than paper and are more pleasing to look at. Recycled paper bedding products work well; they look semi-natural and hold humidity well, although they will eventually mold. If your snake accidentally ingests some, it is easy for the body to pass it without the risk of impaction.

Aspen bedding, a shredded or finely chipped aspen product, is widely available and very appealing aesthetically. Though it holds a certain degree of humidity, it does get moldy in extremely humid conditions and should not be directly misted. This type of bedding is easy to spot-clean.

Cypress mulch and pine bark nuggets are options that hold humidity well and are aesthetically appealing. They are both readily available from garden centers in most areas and are inexpensive. Avoid products sold as "cypress blend," which includes a variety of other species of trees mixed in, some of which might have toxic properties that could harm your snake. Orchid bark is another product that is aesthetically pleasing, but is much more expensive than cypress and pine bark.

Aspen bedding is a fine substrate for a boa cage, but it does not hold humidity very well.

Recycled paper bedding, aspen, cypress mulch, and orchid bark all provide hiding spots for the animals, if deep enough—appropriate substrate depths will vary depending on the size of your animal and style of your enclosure. They may dig in, move around, and pile the substrate, or simply slither beneath it. If you are using any of these products, it will be necessary to feed your animals in a separate enclosure to ensure they do not ingest the substrate (see feeding section, feeding containers).

Soil Substrates

Another substrate choice for keepers that is rapidly gaining popularity is soil. Mixing topsoil, organic potting mix, sand, or peat can give your enclosure a natural appearance. The right mixture will hold humidity well, provide great camouflage and hiding opportunities, and will be easy to spot-clean. Gardening tools (rakes, spades, and shovels) will make cleaning relatively easy. If regular spot cleaning is maintained, complete soil changes are usually only necessary about four times a year for larger cages. Covering your natural dirt substrate with a layer of fallen leaves will greatly increase moisture and will naturally simulate the forest floor. Try collecting leaves on a dry fall day.

Some keepers house their boas on a substrate of leaf litter. Baking this substrate will eliminate any hitchhiking vermin.

A potential downside when using soil and leaf liter is the possibility of parasites or insects coming with the substrate. This can be eliminated or minimized by baking the soil or leaves to remove any stowaways. In the authors' opinion, if your boa is kept properly there should be absolutely no health risk posed by these small insects. Collecting topsoil from clean areas free of pesticides and obvious infestations of insects or mold, or buying sifted dirt from a landscaped yard, will also help eliminate potential problems. If you choose to purchase bags of soil from a garden center, make sure that there are no fertilizers or other potentially harmful additives included in the mixture. Organic potting soil and topsoil may be the best choices.

Substrates to Avoid

Avoid using coarse sand, gravel, or crushed rock as a substrate. Aside from being difficult to clean, it can be abrasive to the snake's skin and can lead to serious intestinal impactions if ingested. Cedar and eucalyptus contain oils that are toxic to reptiles. Do not use substrates containing these woods.

Substrates and Humidity

While maintaining moisture is essential for whatever substrate you choose, too much moisture will invariably cause problems as well, especially with certain types of substrates. Unless you are using newspaper or aspen bedding, which need to stay dry, the substrate should feel barely moist, but not wet. The right amount of ventilation, a large enough water dish, and gentle misting will all help you appropriately achieve adequate humidity levels (60-90 percent). Substrate that is kept too moist will create skin problems for your snake, which can become serious if conditions are not changed immediately.

Light

An incandescent heat lamp provides illumination to the cage so you can see your boa. However, most incandescent bulbs are far from a complete color spectrum, often creating a very yellow cast. If you would like to appreciate you boa's colors to the fullest, a full-spectrum fluorescent bulb can be used to brighten things up. This is a matter of personal preference, however. Since boas do prefer to hide during the daylight hours, providing dark hiding areas is important should your snake want to avoid the bright conditions. Never deny your snake hiding places just so you can see it all the time. Allow it to choose where it wants to be.

Though boas may be hiding during the day, they are most likely aware of the changing of the seasons with the greater amounts of daylight available in the summer and shorter lengths in the winter. The length of daylight time is called the photoperiod. In many animals, changes in the photoperiod will trigger such seasonal activities as hibernation and breeding. For boas, the photoperiod should be maintained at a 12-hour daylight/12-hour darkness regimen. Even if you do not use a light in the cage, snakes will be aware of the seasonal changes through light cast through nearby windows.

Avoid placing cages near a window or otherwise in direct sunlight. The sun shining through a window on a cage even for a short period of time can raise the temperature to harmful levels.

The UV-B wavelength of natural sunlight is necessary for proper nutrition in some other reptiles that are active during the daytime. It is not known if boas would benefit from exposure to natural sunlight or the artificial reptile lights that emit the UV-B wavelength. However, people have been successfully keeping and breeding boas for many years without full spectrum lighting, so it is most likely unnecessary.

Hide Boxes

As mentioned before, boas will need secure hiding spots in their cages. A hide box can be as simple as an appropriately sized terra cotta flower pot or plastic storage box with a hole cut in the side that can be disposed of and replaced when it becomes soiled. A more permanent hide box can be constructed out of wood or other materials. Some keepers prefer to cover their hide boxes with stucco, and paint it to make it look like a natural rock pile. You can be as creative as you like with hiding spots, as long as they are removable, easy to clean, free of sharp edges, and secured in place so the snake doesn't move them around. The hide box should allow your animal's body to touch three or more sides—usually, boas will utilize hiding areas that are smaller than you would expect. Try a few different sizes in multiple heat zones and see which ones they choose.

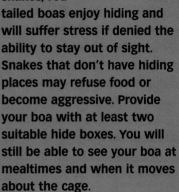

Shy Snakes

Like most snakes, red-tailed boas enjoy hiding and will suffer stress if denied the ability to stay out of sight. Snakes that don't have hiding places may refuse food or become aggressive. Provide your boa with at least two suitable hide boxes. You will still be able to see your boa at mealtimes and when it moves about the cage.

For a more natural look, cork bark is an excellent choice. Cork is harvested mostly in Spain and Portugal, where the thick outer layer of bark is cut off the tree, either in curved

A large piece of cork bark makes an attractive and affordable hide box for a red-tailed boa.

slabs, or tubular hollow branch sections. The tree is not harmed in the process, as another layer of bark will eventually regenerate for a future harvest, making it an environmentally friendly product. Various sizes of curved cork slabs and round, hollow branch sections are often sold specifically for reptile hiding spots at pet shops. Pieces removed from a large branch look exactly like a hollow log, creating a very appealing display. Cork is also very resistant to rot and will not break down in humid conditions. Even very large pieces are lightweight and are unlikely to cause any harm should the snake move them around.

Some companies even manufacture plastic hide boxes of various sizes, some of which are made to look like caves and other natural features. These are perfectly suitable to use and easy to sanitize.

Other Cage Furnishings

Many keepers prefer to add tree branches or driftwood to their setup. Aside from giving the cage a natural look, many boas will climb through the branches, giving them exercise as well as additional objects to rub on when shedding. Putting branches under and around a heat lamp will improve the boa's ability to regulate its temperature by getting up closer to the heat lamp if necessary or down closer to floor level.

Be sure that branches are free of termites and other pests, and that they are not brittle

Escapees

Sometimes, you will encounter a dilemma nobody wants to experience or admit to experiencing—your boa escaped! Don't panic, it won't help you at all. First, check the enclosure to be sure the snake is actually missing (you'd be surprised how well a boa, especially a baby, can hide). Fortunately, boa constrictors do not move quickly. Check around the room, looking for warm dark places where it might like to hide. One escaped boa constrictor was found within the motor compartment of a clothes dryer wrapped around the fan. No wonder the owner complained that the dryer was not working properly (Dowling, 1965)! Most boa constrictors do not venture far from their range, whether found in the wild jungles of Peru or the Cozumel Islands, or within your home.

Of course, it is best if the boa never escapes in the first place. Always secure the cage opening with a lock, and use that lock every time you close the cage.

and likely to break under your snake's weight. Also make sure the branches are secured so they won't shift around as your snake crawls through them, sending your snake crashing down to the floor of the cage. Again, stay away from cedar or any other type of fragrant or potentially toxic wood.

Decorative rocks can be used in the cage, but make sure they are big enough that they won't accidentally be swallowed. On the other hand, make sure they aren't too big and heavy so they won't shift and possibly crush your pet. Avoid stacking rocks to make a hiding area, as your snake's movements will likely cause it to collapse and potentially kill your boa. Again, make sure the rocks you choose do not have sharp edges.

Potted plants may be used as decorative natural accents in your boa's cage. Most plants are only practical in juvenile setups, as adult boas will promptly crush most types of plants. The plant's pot can be concealed behind some rocks or a piece of cork bark, or buried in the substrate. Having plants in a cage can help maintain high humidity levels just from keeping the plant's soil moist. Plants with dense foliage can also create additional hiding spots.

A few easy to care for and readily available potted houseplants, such as the common variegated pothos (*Epipremnum aureum*) and various species of philodendrons (*Philodendron sp.*) can be positioned toward the back of the cage, allowing the vines to hang down and conceal the pot. These species of plant are recommended as they are durable and can tolerate small to medium sized boas crawling over them without crushing them.

Red-Tailed Boas

Your boa's cage will need to be thoroughly cleaned on a monthly basis and spot cleaned as necessary.

For larger enclosures (and larger snakes), you will need to choose plants that are resistant to crushing under the weight of a large boa. Options are limited, but if the cage is tall enough try to choose strong-leaved, upright plants that discourage the snakes from climbing on them, such as small palm trees or other stout trees.

In order to keep the plants healthy, you will need to supply light. A fluorescent light fixture can be purchased from a pet store and used with great results. Standard grow-lights available at hardware stores will work great. Incandescent lights are not preferred by plants, as they are not of a spectrum that plants generally require.

Caging Needs by Age

A baby boa starts life as a small, slender snake, rarely larger than 22 inches long (55.9 cm). In just a few years, that same boa may be over five feet long (1.5 m) and weigh 20 pounds (9.1 kg), and it may reach an eventual length of over 12 feet (3.7 m). Given such an increase in size over the lifetime of a pet boa, the need to adapt the caging for the size and age of the boa is clear.

Cage Maintenance Schedule

Follow this schedule to maintain clean and healthy living conditions for your boa. Never fall behind on these duties, as a dirty cage is inhumane and can lead to severe health problems for your snake and possibly you. These are general guidelines, and certain tasks may need to be done more frequently under certain circumstances.

Every day:

Check to see that the water bowl is clean and free of feces, substrate, algae, scum etc. Thoroughly clean the bowl and refill with clean fresh water if necessary.

Check temperatures in the cage (both the hot spot and the cool spot) and adjust heating or cooling devices when necessary.

Check humidity levels and mist cage with a spray bottle if necessary.

Check the substrate for feces, regurgitations, or any other soiling, and spot-clean as needed.

Remove shed skin if present.

Every week:

Replace newspaper (if used as a substrate).

Clean cage accessories (branches, hide boxes, etc.).

Water any live plants used within the cage.

Thoroughly sanitize water bowl.

Every month:

Completely break down the cage and sanitize with 10 percent bleach solution.

Discard old substrate and add new substrate to clean cage.

Juvenile Caging

A suitably sized enclosure for a juvenile boa is 24-28 inches (61-71 cm) long, 12-24 inches (30.5-61 cm) wide, and 12-24 inches (30.5-61 cm) high. Providing heat for it is as simple as setting up a bulb of correct wattage or an appropriate style of heat pad. Providing humidity may also be as simple as using the right size water dish. Unfortunately, just having the correct size enclosure with adequate heating elements is not enough to start your boa off properly. How you set it up will greatly influence your success or failure.

One of the most important factors when setting up a juvenile boa enclosure is to provide hide spots in the hot and cooler sides of the cage. A variety of hiding spots will allow your boa to tell you if its new environment is sufficient. If the snake is spending all of its time in the hot zone, then it is telling you loud and clear that more heat is needed. Likewise, if it spends most of its time on the cooler side or is constantly cruising the enclosure, then the message is that it's too hot. If not enough hide spots are provided, you will never really know how your boa is doing; it will simply choose the spot it feels secure in and stay there. You may be thinking that with all these hide spots and plants you will never see your boa. This is true only in the beginning; as your snake acclimates, it will go to the first spot it feels comfortable in and stay there for a few hours or a few days.

Subadult Caging

Subadult boas are usually 18 months to 3 years old and 2 to 3 feet (0.6-0.9 m) in length. After properly caring for your animal through the first of its life stages, you will notice its need for more room. Your snake will be increasing in size and you'll need to replace its hide spots two or three times over a year or so. You'll probably see it trying to climb the walls or knocking over its hiding areas or water dish. These are all good indications that a larger enclosure is in order.

The need for a great deal of climbing and exercise should be considered prior to designing or purchasing an enclosure suitable for a subadult. Generally speaking, a good sized cage for subadults is 48 inches (1.2 m) long, 36-48

Handle your boa gently but with confidence. With a large boa, like this Surinam red-tail, supporting as much of the snake as possible is important.

Handling Suggestions

- **Always keep your eyes open and use common sense.**
- **Always keep your snake away from your face, and beware of others around you, especially children.**
- **Approach the snake without hesitation and gently lift it, grabbing it at mid-body.**
- **Never allow a snake to form a complete loop around your neck.**
- **Never handle a large boa (larger than 10 feet/3 m) without assistance.**
- **Never touch prey items before handling your snake; your fingers could be mistaken for food.**
- **Remember that boa constrictors are wild creatures and must be treated with respect.**

inches (0.9-1.2 m) tall, and at least 24 inches (61 cm) wide. One of the authors uses a 48-inch (1.2 m) long, 24-inch (61 cm) wide, and 72-inch (1.8 m) high enclosure, with ventilation on the sides with great success. By adding shelves and drawers to your enclosure, you can provide under and above ground hiding and basking spots. This will allow your animal to choose environments, and increased exercise and movement provided by the extra space will help aid in digestion.

Adult Caging

Housing for adult boas can be a challenge. Unless you plan to force them into a small rack system, there are very few commercially available enclosures of the appropriate size. By the time you have an adult boa, you may have also acquired a mate for it. If you plan on keeping a pair of adults in your home, you should give them the space they require to move comfortably so they are happy and stress-free, and you can enjoy watching their natural behaviors.

An absolute minimum cage floor area for an adult enclosure is 4-6 feet (1.2-1.8 m) long and 24-30 inches (61-76.2 cm) wide. The height of the cage is less critical, but should be at least 3 feet (0.9 m) high. A cage height of 6-8 feet (1.8-2.4 m) combined with suitable branches will allow your boa extra room to climb around, which will give your snake additional exercise. Again, try to get the largest cage you have room for, or at least the biggest you can afford.

Another good way to give your animal room to move about is by building stacking cages. A large boa can live comfortably in an enclosure with a 2 foot x 6 foot (0.6 m x 1.8 m) floor space and 3 or 4 feet (0.9 or1.2 m) of vertical space. This will allow you to put an additional cage on top; the heat from the lower enclosure will help to heat the cage above. With this arrangement, you can use lower wattage heat lamps or tape, saving you money on energy and increasing your overall cage space. Remember, for adults, bigger is always better, more room to move means more enjoyment for them and you. Unfortunately, most keepers seem think that boas do not climb, but this simply is not so.

Cleaning Duties

Cleaning the enclosure is an important chore, but the least enjoyable of your duties as a surrogate snake parent. Learning what routine works best for you, what keeps the snake comfortable and healthy, and what is easy to replace makes this part of reptile husbandry more manageable over the long term.

Excrement, skin sheds, and soiled substrate must be removed daily, if possible, but at least every other day. The water dish should be checked daily and changed whenever dirty.

Every month, a thorough cleansing of the entire enclosure and its contents should be initiated. Enclosure cleaning involves using suitable disinfectants that are nontoxic to reptiles (some disinfectants may be nontoxic to mammals, but toxic to reptiles, so be careful in searching out a proper cleanser). All permanent furnishings of your snake's enclosure (i.e., water bowl, branches, and shelters) should be disinfected as well.

A recommended disinfectant is a 10 percent bleach solution, making sure to rinse off any bleach residue and drying the cleaned surfaces thoroughly before allowing the snake to come into contact with them. Rinse until there is no bleach smell left in the cage or on the furnishings. Bleach is not effective at killing all pathogens, and an additional wipe-down of undiluted ammonia will allow for even more thorough disinfection. Be sure that all bleach residue is removed before applying ammonia, because the reaction between ammonia and bleach releases toxic fumes. Quatenary ammonia disinfectants are also safe to use.

Most boas are docile, but they are wild animals. Use common sense and some caution when handling a boa to avoid being bitten.

Handling

Initially, snake handling is a foreign concept to both the keeper and the kept—it takes time, practice, and great patience to become comfortable with it. A 12-foot (3.7 m) boa can not be safely handled by a single person, and safety is the most important criterion to take into account before dealing with a snake of any size or demeanor. Use your common sense, and with time, experience will teach you when it is a good time to handle a snake. Even the most experienced keepers have let their guard down and have suffered serious bites.

Handling a juvenile for the first time can be a nerve-racking experience if you approach it improperly. Try to be as relaxed as possible. Getting bitten a few times by a small boa will not cause any serious damage. Approach the snake without hesitation and gently lift it, grabbing it at mid-body. The snake should grasp onto your fingers and move from hand to hand. Support as much of the snake's weight as possible; this is especially important with large boas. It is good to keep handling to a minimum until the animal is well acclimated. Taking your boa out a few times a week for short handling sessions will help acquaint you with it.

Snake hooks can be a very helpful tool if you have a particularly aggressive individual or if you are apprehensive about handling your boa, whatever its age or size. Lift the snake with the hook at mid-body, being sure to support it. Do not be surprised if it takes several tries for you and your boa to get used to the process. Never pin the head of the snake with a hook; it can crush its throat and neck bones, causing permanent damage.

When handling large or particularly aggressive snakes, it is wise to have more than one person present. Ideally, with any snake over 12 feet (3.7 m), at least two other people should assist: one to help hold the snake and another to call for help in case of emergency.

Never take your snake out in public. Snakes do not appreciate "going for a walk" and would much rather be left at home. Many laws have been passed banning boa ownership after snake-phobic (ophiophobic) citizens were frightened by them in public

Bites

Receiving a bite from even a subadult can be a painful experience. Theoretically, it is best not to pull your finger or arm away from the snake when bitten, but in practice this can prove to be difficult. Minor bites can be treated with antibacterial soap and triple antibiotic ointment. Occasionally, a few of the snake's teeth may break off in your body. These can usually be easily removed with forceps. Bites from large animals may require a trip to the hospital for stitches.

Argentine boas have a reputation for being snappy.

Most boa bites are the result of improper feeding techniques. Never feed your boa by hand and always wash your hands after handling prey. If you smell like food, you are more likely to get bitten. Boas that are in the blue stage of shedding (when the eyes are a milky blue color) are more likely to bite than they would normally. This is because they cannot see well and feel defensive. It is best not to handle your boa at this time.

Occasionally, a boa may latch on to you and won't let go. This often happens during feeding, when the snake accidentally grabs your hand instead of the food item being offered. When this happens, do not panic and try to pry its mouth open or pull the snake off. Place the open end of a bottle of isopropyl alcohol near its nose, and the smell will instantly make the boa let go. It is a good idea to always keep a bottle of alcohol nearby when handling aggressive snakes. Never pour alcohol on or around the snake's head, as the vapors are enough to irritate the snake.

Chapter 4

Feeding and Growth

Providing proper nutrition for your boa is very important. Boa constrictors are strict carnivores. Because they are usually fed whole animals in captivity (which are generally nutritionally complete), they do not suffer from as many nutritional problems as many other reptiles. However, boas do need to be fed the right way and fed the right prey.

Feeding Schedule

Younger boas should be fed more frequently than older ones and should be offered food every two to three days. Adults should be fed perhaps once a week. This feeding schedule is not set in stone, and there is some degree of flexibility. Snakes in the wild rarely get to eat as often as they do in captivity and may sometimes go for very long periods before catching their prey. That doesn't mean it is okay to not feed your snake for up to a month, and you should definitely try to stick as closely to a feeding schedule as possible. More food should be provided for females prior to breeding and after giving birth. See the feeding chart later in this chapter for a good feeding regimen, which is largely determined by the boa's size.

In nature, boas will feed on any animal they can catch and swallow—in this case, a Mexican free-tailed bat.

Food

Commonly available choices of food for your snake include mice, rats, and—for the largest boas—rabbits and guinea pigs. These are available live or frozen and in a range of sizes.

Prey Size

Proper sizing of food is important. Opinions vary greatly with regard to the proper prey size. Though many snakes can swallow prey much larger than the diameter of their head, dislocating their jaws in the process, there is no need to push the limits of what you feed to your boa. If you are feeding one prey item at a time, select a size with a body diameter that is roughly equivalent to slightly less than the diameter of the snake's midsection. A proper-sized rodent will not create a noticeable bulge in the snake's mid-section after it is ingested. If optimally sized prey is not available, it is always better to err on the smaller side, or to feed more than one rodent of even smaller sizes. Avoid using prey that is too small, though.

Different frozen rodent companies may have different sets of weights for small, medium, and large rodents, and one company's small size may be equivalent to another company's medium size, and yet another company may have a small/medium size. Therefore, it is best to familiarize yourself with the approximate gram weight your boa requires and ask the supplier for something closest to your snake's needs.

Keep the Routine

When purchasing your boa, it's always a good idea to ask how it was being fed so that you can continue its particular feeding regimen. In this way, both you and the snake may be able to avoid some stress during the acclimation process. If you want to change the diet, do so gradually.

Live Food or Frozen?

Rodents are usually available from pet stores and are available live or frozen. Frozen prey is by far the safest and easiest choice. Avoid offering live rodents. When the snake captures the prey, the rodent will become defensive and may bite the snake, which can result in a bad wound and infection.

Although boas can eat very large prey, it is best to feed yours rodents that will not leave more than the slightest bulge in your snake's belly.

Feeding Schedule

Length of Boa	Size & Type of Food	Weekly Feeding
16-24 in. (40-60 cm)	fuzzy mice or pinky rats	1
24-36 in. (0.6-1 meter)	adult mice or fuzzy rats	2-4
3.3 - 4.9 feet (1-1.5 meters)	half-grown rats or chicks	2
4.9-6.6 ft. (1.5-2 meters)	adult rats or half-grown chickens	2
6.6-8.2 ft. (2.0-2.5 meters)	adult rats or half-grown chickens	3 rats or 1-2 chickens
8.2 ft. + (2.5+ meters)	adult rats, chickens, or rabbits	1 rabbit per 3 weeks

From a personal communication with Siar Anthranir.

Uneaten live rodents left in a cage too long have been known to attack and even begin eating the snake, and deaths have occurred when a live rodent is forgotten in the cage. The only time feeding live prey is an option is if the snake will not feed on anything else. This may be the case with imports or some juveniles eating for their first time. Once feeding on live rodents, every effort should be made to transition the snake over to dead prey.

Although it is an option, buying live rodents and prekilling them may be too disturbing for some keepers. Therefore, buying humanely euthanized frozen rodents is much more convenient for most people. If your local pet store does not carry frozen rodents, you can order them from a variety of companies that will deliver them to your door.

Most boas sold today will have been actively feeding on small rodents. A juvenile boa will be large enough to eat pinky rats or fuzzy mice. The term pinky refers to a newborn mouse or rat that does not have hair yet. Fuzzy refers to a newborn mouse or rat that has grown hair but is still not weaned. After a couple of months of regular feeding and growth, your juvenile can graduate to larger prey.

Most keepers try to slowly move from mice to rats, or they exclusively feed rats from the start, as boas will quickly outgrow mice and may be initially reluctant to feed on rats. If your snake is having difficulty transitioning from mice to rats, you can scent the rat by rubbing a mouse on it. Normally this does the trick. Subadults can be fed medium to large rats, and adults of most subspecies will be large enough to take jumbo rats, large guinea pigs, or small rabbits.

Other Prey

There is another feeding option for those who don't want to keep dead rodents in their freezer. A few companies are creating a product marketed as "reptile sausage," which is composed of ground meat (poultry, beef, or other meats) encased in a sausage casing. Experiences vary with this type of product, with some snakes refusing them and others eating them without hesitation. Some companies are trying to refine their products to a more readily accepted, nutritionally complete diet. Right now, these products are more expensive than similarly sized rodents, but they are convenient and more pleasant to use.

Some keepers offer their snakes chicks or chickens depending on the size of the boa. Though chicks may often be cheaper than a similarly sized rodent, rodents are far superior with regard to nutritional completeness. Never feed your boa chicken parts from the meat department of your supermarket. These pieces are not nutritionally complete.

Power Feeding

Power feeding describes the practice of feeding a snake very frequently in order to promote the quickest growth. It is usually employed by breeders to cut down on the time necessary for a snake to reach breeding size. Power feeding is not advised, as it may result in a morbidly obese snake. When your snake is very active, sometimes even during the day, it may be hungry and seeking out food, so watch it and let it tell you what it needs.

How to Feed
Thawing Frozen Prey

When feeding a frozen rodent, allow it to thaw completely to room temperature before offering it to your snake. Allowing a snake to eat a partially thawed or otherwise cold mouse will result in regurgitation or digestive problems. Since the snake is ectothermic, its body will not warm the mouse after it is swallowed and this may have a chilling effect on the snake.

There are several methods to thaw frozen rodents. The easiest is to simply run warm water over it for several minutes until it is thawed out, pat it dry with some paper towels, and then serve it to your boa on tongs. Others prefer to put the frozen rodent in a waterproof zip-lock bag, and soak the bag in a container of warm water. Using this method,

It is safer to feed your boa prekilled rodents—either frozen or freshly killed—than to feed it live prey.

the thawed rodent is dry when removed from the bag, which will reduce the possibility that substrate or other debris will stick to the prey while it is being swallowed. Or you can simply set the frozen rodents out to thaw at room temperature. Again, make sure the rodent is thoroughly thawed and is in no way cold to the touch prior to feeding. Never thaw a frozen rodent in the microwave or heat it in any way to speed the thawing process.

Feeding Procedure

Before offering a snake its meal, always wash your hands so the scent of any handled prey will not get passed on to you, making the snake think you are food, too! Always use the same tongs when feeding (12-24 inch/30.5-61 cm medical hemostats work well for this). Feeding by hand is not a good idea. If the snake misjudges the position of the prey, you could easily be bitten.

Allow your boa to grab hold of the prey with its teeth, and when you are sure it has firmly grasped it, release it. This can be a tricky affair as the snake may coil itself around the tongs by the time you release the prey. It takes practice. Also, when feeding a boa, *never*

Feeding Tools

There are many tools available to the modern herpetoculturist that can aid them in feeding snakes. To successfully keep boas, you will need to acquire the following tools: feeding containers, tongs, and snake hooks. Feeding containers can be anything from a plastic sweater box to a separate cage.

A long pair of tongs (or hemostats) are essential for feeding; they will keep your smell and body heat away from the snake and keep your fingers at a safe distance. You will need to buy bigger, longer tongs as your boa's strike zone increases.

Snake hooks are indispensable, as well. You can use a hook when moving your snake to and from a feeding container. This ensures your safety and greatly reduces the possibility of a feeding-response type of bite.

position your head and eyes at the same level as the snake when it strikes, as it may miss the meal entirely and strike you in the face.

A boa may sense when food is present in the room, and it may be waiting anxiously by the cage door for it to open. Once a snake learns the feeding routine, it will develop a feeding response in which it may blindly strike outward as soon as the cage door is opened. Therefore, caution must be exercised, and all body parts must be kept out of reach of a striking snake.

If the snake misses the prey and latches onto your arm, it might not let go and will start wrapping its body around you, thinking it has just caught the prey it smelled. This will be a very painful experience with larger boas, as their teeth are very long, and it will be very difficult to get the snake to let go. Use the rubbing alcohol method suggested in the previous chapter. Feeding a large boa can be dangerous, and it is best to have someone nearby to help in case of an accidental bite.

Feeding Container

Some keepers choose to feed their boas in a completely separate container from their enclosures. A separate feeding container can be as simple as a plastic sweater box or a clean trash can with a secure-fitting lid, or you can use a different cage altogether. Avoid using bathtubs, bathrooms, or closets for feeding as they are seldom escape-proof and do not keep the animal close enough to the prey item. By feeding your boa in a feeding container, you prevent the snake from forming an association between the opening of a cage and the appearance of food. Using a feeding container can save you a lot of grief and bloodshed when first acclimating your boa. The benefits of using one when keeping more than one boa in the same cage are obvious. Feeding them together is not recommended—one may finish first and pursue the prey item sticking out of its cagemate's mouth, which may result in the head of one of the boas being swallowed!

Using a separate container for feeding your boa can help make feeding more manageable and prevent you from being accidentally bitten.

Fasting

Snakes, boas included, will sometimes go off their food for a time. This should only cause concern if your boa starts losing weight or acting abnormally. In any case, if your boa goes more than a month or so without eating, seek veterinary care.

Problem Feeders

More often than not, a boa that is not feeding probably suffers from an improper husbandry setup. If your boa will not feed, check all husbandry parameters: temperature, humidity, security, etc. If you are satisfied that all conditions are appropriate and your boa still refuses food, there are a few things you can try prior to scheduling a trip to the veterinary office.

Because many boas are nocturnal feeders, you can try leaving your snake in a warm feeding container for several hours before feeding it, then introduce the prey item and leave them in the container overnight.

For stubborn juveniles, you can also try braining the prey items, which means opening up the head and exposing the brain. For some reason, the scent of the brain is enticing enough to get some reluctant feeders to eat, though the technique is not for everyone. Some keepers dip the head of the rodent in condensed chicken broth, the scent of which sometimes appeals to finicky boas.

When you are having difficulty trying to switch the boa from mice to rats, wash a rat with gentle natural soap, rinse, and scent it by rubbing it with a mouse. You can also try freezing a mouse and a rat together, or braining the mouse and smearing the brains on the rat.

Be patient, usually one or a combination of all of these techniques will work for finicky eaters. If your adult boa refuses food for more than a month or two (outside of the breeding season), a trip to a qualified reptile veterinarian is highly recommended. If the snake is a juvenile, you should seek veterinary attention sooner.

Shedding Myths

Skin shedding is called ecdysis. A snake usually sheds its skin in its entirety. Many myths and legends centered on the immortality of snakes probably originated because of their ability to shed their skins, which evokes the image of a new life. Of course, snakes do not shed their skins to begin new lives but to continue their old ones.

Excrement

For all animals and plants, what goes in must come out. For reptiles, much of what is ingested is processed and eliminated as waste. Reptiles have a different excretory system than higher mammals; their wastes are composed of mainly two different substances: uric acid and feces. In reptile excrement, uric acid is white, sometimes chalky in appearance; it is an insoluble by-product of the kidneys and is essentially concentrated solid urine. Occasionally, some liquid is also dispelled from the cloaca. All of this is a normal part of the elimination process. Although it isn't pleasant, it's a good idea to become familiar with the appearance of your boa's normal stool. This will give you a chance to spot changes that could signal a health problem.

Growth and Shedding

The boa constrictor grows fastest during its formative first year, then slows afterwards. It does continue to grow during its entire lifetime. A newborn boa constrictor may double its body weight in 45 days, and can triple its body weight in 60 days under optimal conditions.

With proper care, a red-tailed boa will grow quickly. It may grow over 3 feet (0.9 m) in the first year of life.

During the first year, the boa may have gained 17 to 22 times its birth weight; during the second year, it may gain (only!) 53-72 percent of its first year weight (Herfs, 1959). A ballpark figure for the growth rate of a regularly fed *Boa constrictor imperator* may often be 4-5 feet (1.2-1.5 m) total length in a calendar year. A female may reach 12 feet (3.7 m) in total length within a 4-5 year period. So, relatively speaking, boa constrictors are fast growing reptiles. Of course, optimal temperature ranges and good husbandry practices increase growth rates in captive snakes.

It is not easy to provide a standard rate of growth for the boa constrictor, as so many factors contribute to it. The measure of your own animal's growth may be easier to calculate by how many skin sheds it has per year—the more skin that is shed annually, the faster your boa has grown in that calendar year. But how many skin sheds can one expect within a 12-month period? Young boas grow faster; hence, they should have more frequent skin sheds than, say, a 10-foot (3 m) adult. When young, a boa constrictor can shed its entire skin every six weeks.

The lifespan of your boa is directly related to the care you provide it. Common sense will tell you that a well-cared for boa will live a longer life than one that is not well-cared for. Boas have been known to live for at least 30 years when properly taken care of.

When shedding is approaching, the snake may take refuge in a quiet place. The snake may appear to take on a milky blue/grey cast, especially noticeable in the eyes. Snakes in this condition are sometimes referred to as "opaque" or "in blue." Because snakes cannot see well when they are opaque, they may be defensive and more prone to bite. It is best to avoid handling them at this time.

A day or two before shedding takes place, this coloration will disappear. Then shedding will occur, normally taking from less than an hour to more than a day, depending on the size of the snake. The snake may often be seen rubbing its head on cage furnishings to loosen the skin from around the lips. Once the shedding is completed and the skin is sloughed off, the snake will resume its daily activities, with feeding being one of its first priorities. Remove the cast off skin as soon as you notice it.

Size

Some boa constrictors have been reported to attain almost monstrous size according to some observers. In the past, there have been reports of boa constrictors reaching up to 30 feet in total length (4.3-9.1 m). Today, boa constrictors of these dimensions are considered exaggerations or a result of misidentifying the species, and in many instances probably apply to the anaconda (*Eunectes murinus*). The average adult boa constrictor ranges from 5-7 feet (1.5-2.1 m) long (Campbell, 1998). The species' maximum length is somewhere in the 12-foot range (3.7 m). William Beebe and his guide Degas collected the largest wild-caught, live-measured specimen on June 28, 1922, when they caught a sizeable 12-foot, 6-inch (3.8 m) boa constrictor near Kartabo, Venezuela, prior to its shipment to the New York Zoological Park (Bronx Zoo) in New York City (Beebe, 1946).

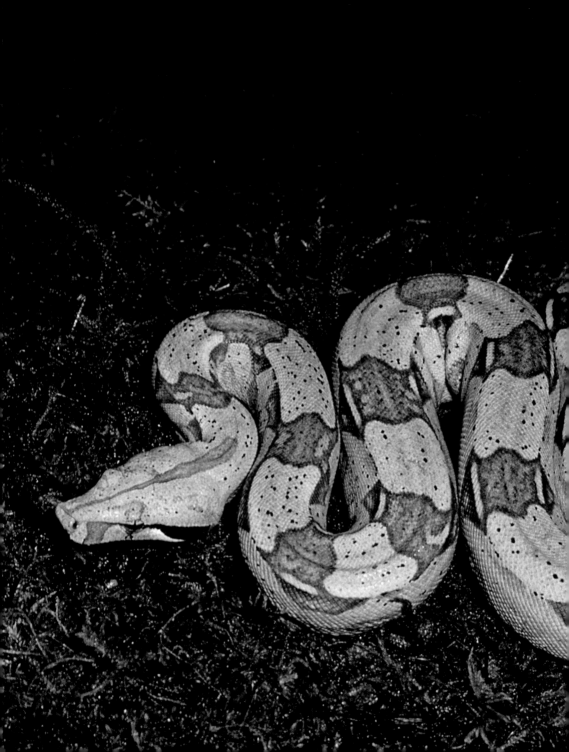

Chapter 5

Breeding

After you have mastered the art of boa keeping, you may decide to take the next step and breed your boas. In addition to the fun of producing your own baby boas, there are many reasons why you may want to breed your snakes. Breeding your snakes is a great learning experience for all ages. It is quite an experience to see a female boa giving birth to a large litter of live young, even if you have experience with hatching other species of snakes from eggs. Maybe you would like to make some money selling your offspring. Making healthy captive-bred reptiles available reduces the need to collect from wild populations.

There are many different color phases and pattern morphs that have surfaced through mixing and matching different individuals. Selective breeding to emphasize traits is fun to do, and mixing different colors or patterns is a fun way of learning genetics. Perhaps you will end up with a new morph that every serious reptile enthusiast will be willing to pay a high price for!

Breeding Considerations

Before setting forth with plans to breed your animals, make sure you are prepared. Breeding the more popular, easy-to-keep subspecies may

Interesting colors and patterns are found in wild boas frequently. This mahogany-colored boa could start a new morph.

seem as simple as putting a male and female together and waiting for them to do their thing. Often it is that simple, as long as the animals are healthy and kept in an acceptable environment. But, will you be prepared for the litter of babies? Will you be ready to properly care for the babies when they are born? Do you have a plan to find new homes for the offspring you do not wish to keep?

In addition to housing the breeders, you will need to anticipate how many offspring you may end up producing and plan on how you will house them all. One boa may give birth to well over 50 babies in a litter. You will need to make sure ahead of time that you have all the additional equipment necessary for properly maintaining temperatures and other parameters for the neonates.

If you are attached to the animals you intend to breed, be aware that breeding increases the risk of serious and even fatal health problems among your boas. All potential breeders must have excellent body weight. A snake whose health is borderline will quickly begin

Recordkeeping

It is extremely important to keep good records from the time you breed your snakes together to the time the neonates are feeding. Devising a recordkeeping system and maintaining accurate records are vital to success. This can be as simple as data cards with handwritten information to a computer database.

Information such as the names or ID numbers of the parents, their origins, breeding date, color of parents, and other relevant details should be recorded in some way from the beginning. During the course of your female's pregnancy, any significant events that arise should be recorded along with the date observed. These events would include accidental temperature fluctuations, health issues, sheds, etc. This information can allow you to gradually learn if the conditions you are providing are leading to success or failure.

By knowing the date the female successfully copulated and keeping track of the gravid female's shed cycles, you will be able to predict approximately when the young will be born. This will allow you to prepare in advance for housing the babies. The birthdates of the babies should be recorded, and each baby should be assigned an ID number. Individual records can be kept from day one tracking important data such as feeding and shedding dates. Providing this information to those who buy your babies will show that you are a dedicated and trustworthy herpetoculturist.

wasting away when subjected to the stress of breeding and giving birth. Complications may result that may jeopardize the health of the mother and the babies. Make sure two snakes of the opposite sex have been properly quarantined for a suitable length of time prior to putting them together for breeding. You don't want your pregnant female catching a serious disease from the male she bred with.

You will need to be ready with a steady supply of properly sized food items. Make sure you plan ahead with others who may be interested in acquiring some offspring from you. That way, when you are sure your babies are healthy and feeding, you won't need to take care of them for longer than you need to. If you will be shipping your hatchlings to their new owners, familiarize yourself with the proper way of shipping live reptiles and dealing with temperature extremes during transit. Check with the carrier to see if they have any restrictions with shipping live reptiles.

Sexing

Before you can breed your boas, you obviously need to confirm that you have two animals of the opposite sex. There are several methods for sexing a boa, and some are more reliable than others. Some methods can cause harm or permanent damage to your snakes if done incorrectly. It is highly recommended that you are taught these techniques by an experienced breeder in person, rather than learning them through trial and error. You wouldn't want to render your snake unable to reproduce when that is your goal in the first place.

Male snakes have a pair of copulatory organs called *hemipenes* (singular = *hemipenis*). When the snake is not mating, these structures are kept inverted in the base of the tail behind the vent. These function similarly to a penis in male mammals as a means of transferring sperm to the female. Though the snake has two hemipenes, only one is used during mating. One method of sexing a boa is by attempting to manually evert the hemipenal structures. If the snake is a male, the hemipenes will be pushed out the vent and will be clearly visible. If it is a female, no hemipenes will be everted. This is an unreliable method for the inexperienced, and again, can result in permanent damage to the snake's hemipenes, as well as damage to the bones in the tail if too much pressure is applied. This inspection is easier to perform on younger boa constrictors than large adults because the muscles that hold the hemipenes in place are much stronger in the larger animals.

Boas have a pair of claws (spurs) on each side of the vent. These are evidence that the ancestors of snakes had legs millions of years ago, and they gradually became reduced to a point where all that remains are these claws and some internal skeletal remnants of a pelvis. In general these spurs are often more prominent in males than in females, but even among males there are variations in spur size. Male snakes use the spurs in courtship behavior.

Table 6: Determining the Sex of Boas by Depth of Probe in Subcaudal Scales

Species	Male	Female
Boa constrictor constrictor	10-12	2-3
Boa constrictor amarali	9	3-4
Boa constrictor imperator	10	3-4
Boa constrictor occidentalis	10-11	3
Boa constrictor orophias	10-12	2-4
Boa constrictor ortonii	10-12	4

Most boas will become sexually mature at a size of 4.5-6 feet (1.4-1.8 m), but the dwarf varieties, like Hog Island boas, mature at much smaller sizes.

Another method of sexing snakes is by examining them with sexing probes. These instruments are basically straight rods of stainless steel with rounded tips that are available in different diameters for different sizes of snakes. These are available from some breeders and specialty pet supply stores. This procedure is also very risky and is best taught by an experienced person. Probe size is extremely important, as a probe that is too small will pierce a hole in the fragile hemipenis, causing your boa great pain and rendering the hemipenis useless and possibly creating a serious infection.

A water-soluble lubricant is applied to the probe, and it is inserted into the snake's vent and angled down into the base of the tail. If your snake is a male, the probe will insert further into the tail base (into one of the inverted hemipenes) than in a female. Females do have a shallow pocket that the probe will insert into, but it will not go as deep as in a male. Using the scales on the underside of the tail (subcaudal scales) starting behind the vent as a measurement of probe depth, a female will probe to a depth of two to four subcaudal scales. Adult males probe to a depth of about 10-12 subcaudal scales, and neonate male boa constrictors probe to a depth of perhaps 7-8 subcaudal scales (Ross, 1990; de Vosjoli, 1990; Divers, 1996). Sexing adult boa constrictors is a two-person effort, as the boa in question may strongly object to your invasive probing of its cloaca region. Be prepared.

Sexual Maturity

Sexual maturity is that period of time when an animal becomes able to reproduce. For the red-tailed boa, it is not so much age but size that establishes when this species may breed. Most boas will become mature at a size of 4.5-6 feet (1.4-1.8 m) in total length, which is usually at around 4 or 5 years of age.

It is best to be patient and not force a barely mature snake to breed. If a female breeds and is not large enough, she may experience a problem in which she is unable to give birth to her young, a condition known as dystocia. Also, younger females will usually have a smaller litter size than larger adults.

Breeding is an extremely stressful event for any female, red-tailed boas included. When preparing your adults, make sure they are healthy animals, as this is an important prerequisite for a safe and successful breeding event. Make sure the female is fed well prior to breeding and is of a good body weight. During gestation she will go off feed for weeks or months, drinking water intermittently. She will need to have the fat and nutrient reserves to not only produce young but also maintain her own health during this fasting.

Temperature and Reproduction

Many other commonly bred snake species in the pet trade that originate from temperate regions will often require a winter cooling (brumation) period into at least the 50°F (10°C) range to stimulate breeding in spring. Boas, however, come from regions without drastic seasonal temperature changes. Cooling a boa like you would a king snake or a rat snake could be fatal. Snakes from temperate regions may also be aware of seasonal changes with the changes in photoperiod throughout the year, with shorter amounts of daylight in winter and longer periods of daylight in summer. Within the range of the boa's distribution, the daily photoperiod averages roughly 12 hours of daylight and 12 hours of night year-round.

Knowing this information, what is it that determines a boa's breeding cycle? Are there any environmental cues to signal the snake that it is time to reproduce? Seasonal changes in the tropical haunts of boas do include minor temperature changes, as well as fluctuations in rainfall amounts over the course of the year. These factors appear to be the triggering signals that induce reproductive behavior (Andrews, 1996; Divers, 1996; Ronne, 1996; Fogel, 1997).

Opinions vary greatly when it comes to the temperature breeder boas should be exposed to, as well as the duration of time they are kept in these temperatures. Many breeders recommend dropping the nighttime temperatures into the low 70s (about 21.1-22.8°C). Others have had success with only slight temperature drops. Some breeders only keep it this cool for a few weeks. Others recommended that this cool-down period be maintained up to10 weeks before returning to an ambient temperature of 86°-90°F (30°-32°C) (Divers, 1996; see Tables 6-7). Some breeders keep a warm spot available during the cool times, while others do not give their snakes a choice and force them to be exposed to temperatures in the low 80s (about 26.7-28.3°C) during the day and low 70s (about 21.1-22.8°C) during the night. A few people have successfully bred their snakes without any temperature changes at all.

So with all these varying opinions, how does one choose a method to use? This data may show that boas may not be as particular to the length of the cooling period, as long as they experience at least several weeks of it. Therefore, it is less risky for the animals to cool them for a shorter length of time. Three to four weeks might be all that is necessary to successfully breed your boas.

During cooling, the snakes should be closely monitored as they are more susceptible to

Breeders create new varieties by breeding boas that exhibit interesting traits. For example, this boa has a reduced pattern and pinkish sides which it could pass on to its offspring.

Don't Breed a Skinny Boa

Ensuring that your breeding pair has excellent body weight prior to cooling can not be stressed enough. A healthy, plump boa will have no problem surviving a month without eating, and weight loss during this time will be minimal and barely noticeable. If your boas are underweight, fatten them up and breed them next year.

respiratory infections in cool conditions. If you hear wheezing or whistling noises as your snake breathes, or if you see foaming at the mouth, immediately warm the snakes' temperatures up and keep them warm. Seek the help of your veterinarian for treatment.

With reduced temperatures, digestion slows down considerably. Any food in their digestive tracts could putrefy and cause serious illness. Therefore, it is best to not feed your boas during their cool period and to withhold food for about two weeks before breeding.

Mating

After making sure your breeders are healthy and of good body weight, and they have undergone a period of reduced temperatures, it is time to warm them up, begin feeding again, and begin the courting and mating process. It is best that the first meal after cooling be on the small side, as the body may have trouble adjusting to a large prey item again.

Begin by putting the male and the female together. Some breeders prefer to put the female in the male's cage, assuming he will be confused in the female's cage with everything smelling like her. Tail lifting and cloacal gaping are indications that the female is receptive. Boa constrictors use pheromones to broadcast their readiness to mate, and these chemical cues enable the male and female boas to discriminate one another.

Some breeders keep the pair together for days to weeks at a time, separating them only to feed them, while others will keep the pair together overnight, separating them the following day and reintroducing them several more times over the upcoming weeks. There are advantages to both of these methods, and whichever you chose is a matter of personal preference.

Males begin with courtship behavior often weeks before females do. In this way, they may "woo" the females into initiating ovulation. Courtship behavior may occur for several hours to several days, depending on the female's receptiveness to mating. During ovulation, the female's body will appear swollen from the midsection to just before the vent.

Mating pair of *B. c. imperator*. Note the entwined tails.

Sometimes, she will twist her body so the ventral or lateral side faces upward. When you note your adult female twisting in this manner, you know she is ready for mating.

Mating behavior ensues when the male aligns his body parallel to the female's body and entwines his tail with the female's, with their heads usually adjacent to one another. Their tails are lifted up slightly, and one of the male's copulatory organs is then inserted into the female. The male's tail may be observed waving in the air as copulation takes place. Seminal fluid is then transferred inside the female's cloaca for fertilization.

Brooding Chambers

Courting adult boa constrictors can be kept in a 4 foot x 3 foot x 3 foot (1.2 m x 0.9 m x 0.9 m) terrarium, which provides ample room for the snakes and easy access for the keeper. Brooding chambers such as this can be kept around 80°- 85°F (26.7°-29.4°C) at a cooler end, with a warmer end reaching 92°F (33.3°C). Food can be offered every two to three days, separating the pair temporarily at that time. Once mating has successfully ensued, remove the male and leave the female alone as much as possible, keeping interruptions limited to cleaning the brood chamber and occasional checkups.

Gestation

After the pair has been together several times over the course of several weeks, the female is hopefully in the early stages of pregnancy—usually called *gravidity* when referring to reptiles. Gestation may last from as little as four months to as long as eight or more months. The time between a successful mating and fertilization may vary as well, as females of many species of reptile are known to have the ability to retain sperm for long periods, and they can use it to fertilize their ova when they feel conditions are right. Therefore, exact gestation time from fertilization to birth is nearly impossible to predict. A variety of factors, including temperature during gestation and the female's genetics may also contribute to the length of gestation.

During gestation, it is important to keep the female at a constant temperature. If temperatures fluctuate, deformities or stillborns may result. You should also continue to offer the female food. Some pregnant females may be reluctant to feed, but others will continue to feed without hesitation. Try offering smaller than usual prey items to reluctant females. If you can't get the female to eat, don't worry—as long as she went into breeding with good body weight, she will be able to cope with the remainder of the process.

Towards the end of the gestation period, the female will become noticeably swollen in the rear half of her body. It is important to avoid picking her up at this time, as this may damage the developing fetuses within her.

Prior to giving birth, a female boa will shed her skin. When this happens, you should start preparing your caging for the neonates. The mother will normally give birth within three weeks after she sheds.

Invasion of the Boas

Recently, populations of wild-caught *Boa constrictor imperator* have become established in the urban area of Miami, Florida. This is mainly due to irresponsible pet owners who release their pets after they have gotten too big to deal with. They appear to be breeding there, as U.S. Fish & Game officials have caught multiple gravid females, neonates, and boas of all sizes within and around this city (Bartlett, 2003; R. & S. Pierre, pers. obs.). Remember to never let your boas go. If you can't keep them or sell them, give them to a new owner or a reptile rescue.

Neonates

Females may give birth to litters ranging in number from single digits to well over 60 babies. When first born, each neonate is encased in a clear membrane attached to a yolk sac. The boa will break through the membrane and detach itself from the yolk sack and begin crawling around. The birthing process is messy and may be a little bloody, but this is normal.

Among any given litter of snakes, 1 to 5 percent of the litter can be stillborn, which is considered normal. In many cases, stillborns occur later in the pregnancy when the babies are nearly fully formed. Rough handling and undue stress to the mother, egg turning, and temperature failure can also be causes of such events. If you are worried your pregnant female boa might be having some problems during her pregnancy, an ultrasound performed by your vet might help discern what, if anything, is occurring that might be detrimental to her.

Boas are born in a thin sac that ruptures during birth or shortly thereafter.

Not all of the female's eggs may be successfully fertilized. During the birthing process, a few infertile eggs (often referred to as "slugs") may be deposited along with the babies. These usually appear as soft, solidified yellowish masses. A few mixed with an otherwise good litter is normal, but a high number of slugs may indicate fertility problems with the male or female or improper conditions during the breeding process.

Sometimes babies may be born with deformities. These often include spinal kinks, misshapen heads, shortened lower jaws, etc. Unless the deformity is very minor, rarely do these babies survive, and they are best euthanized by your veterinarian as soon as possible. Other babies may be perfectly formed, but exhibit unusual patterning or coloration. All of these anomalies are attributed to incorrect gestation temperatures, poor handling of females, and genetics.

When the babies are born, they measure approximately 14-18 inches (35.6-45.7 cm).

Genotype vs. Phenotype

The terms genotype and phenotype often come up when discussing the selective breeding of animals. The two terms are different but related. The genotype is the actual genetic makeup of an organism, as distinguished from its physical appearance. The phenotype is the observable physical and/or biochemical characteristics of an organism, as determined by genetics and environmental factors. Thus, the genotype determines the phenotype.

They exhibit little sexual dimorphism in size or weight at this age, but are usually more brightly marked than their parents—a common occurrence seen among many reptiles.

After the neonates are born, they are entirely on their own. The mother provides no additional care for them. They should be collected from the mother's cage immediately after being born and set up individually in their own cages. High humidity is important for newly hatched boas. Several days after birth, they go through their first shed. After successfully shedding, they are ready to begin feeding.

Boa Color Morphs and Selective Breeding

Over the years, many new and interesting colors of red-tailed boas have become available to the pet trade. Many of these colors are inheritable genetic traits that can be perpetuated through selective breeding. Breeders are mixing and matching the various color and pattern variations together to produce even more new and desirable variants. Adding some of these unique colors to your boa collection and starting a selective breeding project may be the next desired step for experienced boa keepers.

When determining the best breeding project for you, it would be best to start with a trait that is definitely inheritable. This means that if you breed two parents together who are both gene carriers for the same trait, they will have a certain number of offspring displaying that trait. Some traits are not yet proven to be genetic, and others, such as striped boas, can be genetic or the result of other factors. Many of the most unusual traits are highly desirable and still not readily available; therefore, they command high prices. Some of these projects may be great investments.

Simple Recessive Traits

Boas, like most animals, receive half their genetic makeup from each parent. For each gene, the boa gets a copy of that gene (called an *allele*) from each parent. Each allele may code for a different expression of a trait, such as normal coloration and amelanistic coloration (often called albino). In some cases—as in amelanism—one allele may hide the presence of the other. When this is true, the hidden trait is called recessive and the other is called dominant.

The point of understanding dominant and recessive traits is realizing that the parents don't need to be visually displaying a desired trait in order to produce offspring that display the trait. Let's use the albino trait as an example. Albinism, or amelanism, is a term used for a mutation that is characterized by the elimination of melanin, a black pigment that gives animals their dark colors. Not having any melanin, amelanistic boas have a very light appearance composed of pink, yellow, and white shades, which are basically the remaining pigments in the snake's skin. Amelanism is a known simple recessive trait.

If you breed a boa that is visibly amelanistic to another boa that is also visibly amelanistic, their offspring will be all be amelanistic. On the other hand, if you breed a visible amelanistic boa to a normal-appearing boa that is not a gene carrier for amelanism, you will get all normal-appearing boas. However, all of these offspring will be gene carriers for albinism. These offspring are referred to as *heterozygous*, or

Here is a newly born litter of boas along with some slugs (unfertilized ova). Given the mix of albino and normally colored babies, one of the parents was not albino.

sometimes simply referred to as *het* for albinism. If both genes are the same (either the dominant or recessive form), the boa is considered to be *homozygous*. A recessive trait will only be displayed if the individual is homozygous.

If you raise these normal appearing babies that are het for albinism and breed two of them together, you will end up with 25 percent of the babies appearing amelanistic, 25 percent will be normal and *not* het for amelanism, and 50 percent will be normal appearing and *be* het for albinism. Since 75 percent of the babies will appear normal, you won't be able to tell which ones are heterozygous and which aren't. Therefore, babies from this type of breeding are often sold as "66 percent possible het for amelanism," since two-thirds of the normal appearing boas will be hets. This means that if you buy one of these normal-appearing boas from this litter, you have a 66 percent chance that your boa is heterozygous for amelanism.

If you breed a normal-appearing boa that is het for albinism to another boa that is visually albino, you will end up with 50 percent of the babies visually albino, and 50 percent normal-appearing but definite hets for albinism. See the table below for a visual representation.

If you breed a boa that is normal-appearing but heterozygous for amelanism to another boa that is normal-appearing and not het for amelanism, you will end up with all normal-appearing offspring, but 50 percent of these will be het for amelanism, and 50 percent will

Example Cross With One Recessive Trait

	Male Gene A	Male Gene a
Female Gene A	AA **Present in 25% of young** **(No recessive genes)**	Aa **Present in 25% of young** **(Heterozygous: Carries desired gene, but does not show it)**
Female Gene a	Aa **Present in 25% of young** **(Heterozygous: Carries desired gene, but does not show it)**	aa **Present in 25% of young** **(Homozygous: Displays desired recessive traits)**

not be het for amelanism. Since it is unknown which babies are het and which aren't, babies from this type of breeding are sold as "50 percent possible het for albinism," meaning you have a 50 percent chance that one of the normal-appearing babies is a definite het.

Knowing his information, you will understand why heterozygous animals are less expensive than homozygous animals. You will also understand why possible hets are even more inexpensive than definite hets, being that you risk the chance that your snake is not heterozygous for the desired trait.

Amelanism As mentioned earlier, albino or amelanistic animals lack the black pigment melanin. There are at least two different genetic mutations that cause amelanism, each often referred to as a *bloodline* in the hobby. They look very similar, but have differences in the amount of various colors displayed. The main difference between these bloodlines is that, when bred together, you won't get an albino snake. Breeding two amelanistic boas of separate strains together will result in normal-appearing boas

Hypomelanism is a codominant mutation that reduces the amount of black pigment in the skin, allowing more red to be seen.

that are 100 percent heterozygous for both types of amelanism, often called a *double het*. If you raise up and breed these double hets, you will get a mix of genotypes ranging from normal boas, to those expressing one of the forms of amelanism, to ones homozygous for both forms (the latter should be one-sixteenth of the babies).

Anerythrism Anerythristic animals lack the red pigment erythrin. As with amelanism, there are several strains of anerythrism known. Anerythristic boas look their best as juveniles, and with the red pigment gone, all that is left is a very pleasing black and silver coloration. In some of the strains, this coloration gains more brown coloration as the snake matures.

Codominant Traits

Some boa mutations work a little differently than simple recessive traits. Codominant traits are unusual in that you can breed a boa displaying the trait to another normal boa that is not a gene carrier for the particular trait, and the resulting offspring will contain some babies visibly displaying the codominant trait. As an added bonus, breeding two of these boas displaying the codominant trait will result in offspring exhibiting a more refined and even more visually appealing appearance, which is the dominant or so-called "super" form of the trait.

Therefore, individuals heterozygous for a codominant trait of the dominant form are clearly displaying the desired characteristics, although not in as dramatic a form as the homozygous individuals. For the beginning boa morph breeder, codominant traits are fun since there is instant gratification in the first season of breeding.

Hypomelanism Hypomelanism is an example of a codominant trait. Hypomelanism (often call hypo) is the reduction of the black pigment melanin, but not a complete absence as in amelanism. Since the boas still have some black pigment, the resulting appearance is a very pleasing lightly colored version of the normal form. Areas that would normally be a muddy brown in normal boas appear light tan to even orange in hypomelanistic specimens.

If you breed a boa displaying the hypo trait to a normal boa that is not a gene carrier for hypomelanism, then 50 percent of the offspring will be normal-appearing and non-gene carriers for the hypomelanistic trait, while the other 50 percent will appear hypomelanistic.

If two of these boas displaying hypomelanism are bred together, the resulting offspring will be 50 percent hypo, 25 percent normal non-gene carriers, and 25 percent super-hypo, which is the dominant form of the hypo trait. Gene carriers for codominant traits will never have normal coloration, as they do in simple recessive traits.

A super-hypo bred to a hypo (homozygous to heterozygous forms) will yield half hypo and half super-hypo offspring. A dominant super-hypo bred to a normal, non-gene carrier will yield 100 percent codominant hypos. Two super-hypos bred together (homozygous to homozygous) will result in 100 percent super-hypos.

Other Codominant Traits Other than hypomelanism, there are several other codominant traits becoming more and more available. Hypomelanism affects the snake's color, but there are also traits that affect the snake's patterning. These include arabesque (heavy black pattern with saddles connected), jungle, and motley, all of which are codominant traits.

Mixing and Matching

The fun of creating new and unusual colors and patterns can be taken to the next level by combining various traits. Often these combinations can result in some very unusual-appearing snakes that would never be otherwise seen in nature. Snow boas are an example of a combination of recessive traits.

Some breeders work with boas from certain parts of the range and breed to maintain these lines. This is a captive-bred *B. c. constrictor* from northern Brazilian stock.

Snow Boas A snow boa is created when amelanism and anerythrism are both displayed by a boa at the same time. The boa is homozygous for both traits, or double homozygous. With the black and red pigments gone in the same snake, various shades of white and light yellow are left, with patterning faintly visible. A snow boa is made by breeding an amelanistic boa to an anerythristic boa. Knowing how simple recessive traits work, the offspring from this breeding will all be normal-appearing, but all will be gene carriers for the two traits, or double het. Breeding these double hets together will result in a percentage of the litter being snow boas. Breeding two snows together (double homozygous and double homozygous) will result in all offspring being double homozygous.

Other Combinations There are many possibilities when mixing and matching the above described colors and patterns. Codominant and recessive traits can be combined. Amelanism, hypomelanism, and anerythrism, which are all color mutations, can be combined with pattern mutations to make things like amelanistic motleys, hypo arabesques, and anerythristic jungles. Combining hypomelanism with anerythrism creates ghost boas. As

Starting a Selective Breeding Project

In order to manage a selective breeding project, you will need to be able to keep accurate and detailed records so you can remember who the parents of a particular snake were, what traits it might be a gene carrier for, etc.

One danger of selective breeding is the possibility of inbreeding. This is not usually a problem in early stages of breeding closely related boas to each other, but it can eventually be a problem if new genetics aren't being regularly added to keep future generations genetically diverse. Results of inbreeding are most noticeably developmental deformations, though seemingly normal-appearing yet inbred animals may have other less noticeable undesirable features, including low fertility or weak health.

For best results, make sure you are working with a diverse initial stock from the beginning. Select as many females as you can that display the traits you want to work toward emphasizing, and breed the best males you can find with these traits. Try to do your best to obtain females from various sources. It is important to keep records on the parentage of the offspring, as you will want to avoid regular inbreeding in one lineage. Breeding two exceptionally colored siblings together, or breeding a hatchling to its parent, is unlikely to cause problems, but care must be taken to not keep breeding resulting generations together again. Mixing new genetics into the project, known as out-breeding, is very beneficial.

mentioned above, anerythrism results in a black and silver snake, and then if the melanin is reduced by the hypo gene, the result is the faded, light gray and silver coloration of the ghost boa. Amelanism and hypomelanism can be combined to produce a sunglow, a bright orange, white, and red boa.

As more and more people are breeding boas and mixing in new bloodlines, new and interesting things continue to pop up. Perhaps one day there will be as many boa morphs as there currently are morphs of corn snakes and ball pythons.

Chapter 6

Health Care

Proper husbandry and preventive care are essential to your red-tailed boa's health and longevity. The first thing any responsible keeper should do following the purchase of a new snake is take it to a qualified reptile veterinarian for an examination. A good physical should include a basic fecal exam and a thorough check of its overall condition. Once your boa is in its new home, it is important to keep in mind that most health problems can be avoided with proper care. Also, a yearly visit to the vet is assurance that your pet will stay healthy.

Health problems in a boa may show themselves in several ways. Changes in a snake's behavior are always a good indication that it could be sick. A boa may have a change in disposition, a refusal to eat, as well as changes in habits like basking or frequenting favorite hiding areas, etc. Changes in appearance may also signal a problem and include sunken eyes, weight loss, swollen areas, changes in skin other than shedding, abnormal feces, etc. If you think your snake is sick and you aren't sure what to do, it's always a good idea to consult your veterinarian before conditions worsen. Quite often, many illnesses can only be correctly diagnosed and treated by a vet.

Aside from proper husbandry issues, all reptiles should be kept away from potentially toxic substances. Cigarette smoke is obviously bad for humans, and can be worse for reptiles. Chemical fumes, such as those produced from aerosol insecticides, air fresheners, perfumes, and household cleaners, should not be used in the same room your boa is in. After using cleaning chemicals such as bleach to clean cages or cage furnishings, make sure to thoroughly rinse all residue off so there is no chance that your animals will come in contact with it.

Injuries can be avoided by making sure all cages and their furnishings are safe. Make sure there are no rough-cut materials in the cage. Sharp edges can catch on skin and create tears, especially on the delicate skin of juveniles. Metal hardware cloth or metal screen incorporated in the cage's construction can be abrasive to snakes that may end up rubbing their noses on it. The edges of these types of mesh are sharp and should be concealed. Optimally, metal screen or hardware cloth is not recommended. To prevent burns, make sure your snakes are unable to come in direct contact with hot light bulbs.

Proper husbandry is the key to making sure your boa stays healthy.

Finding a Suitable Vet

As pet reptiles become increasingly popular, the number of veterinarians with at least basic knowledge of reptile medicine continues to grow. Still, it is a difficult task to find a veterinarian with proper experience. Many vets still specialize only in traditional pets such as dogs and cats and other popular warm-blooded animals. Don't necessarily go with a vet who may claim to have experience treating reptiles, as their experiences may be very limited. The many negative experiences from keepers clearly show that there are too many vets who accept reptile patients yet really don't know what they are doing. Of course, with diligent searching, you can find vets that are knowledgeable, yet even the experts may not have the answers to everything, as herpetological medicine has, until recently, been an area that has not received enough attention.

A good way to find a vet educated in reptile medicine is to search the listings of members on the webpage of the Association of Reptile and Amphibian Veterinarians (ARAV). The website for the ARAV is www.arav.org. There you can find the closest vet to you who is a member, and therefore up to date on the latest in proper reptile care. The ARAV is dedicated to improving reptilian veterinary care and husbandry through research and education.

Be sure there are no electrical wires or components exposed in the cage. Materials such as rocks, branches, or other heavy cage furnishings need to be secured so they don't move, but not in a way that they can't be removed for cleaning. These materials can shift and fall, injuring or even killing an inhabitant.

Reptile Veterinarians

Before problems arise, you should seek out a veterinarian with reptile experience in your area. Unfortunately, veterinarians with knowledge of proper reptile husbandry and medicine are few and far between. This has been slowly changing as reptiles have become more popular and accepted as mainstream pets in recent years. Pet stores that sell reptiles can often recommend veterinarians, as well as fellow hobbyists in your area. It is worth traveling the extra distance and/or spending more money for good care and advice that may otherwise mean life or death for your pet.

Quarantine

All new acquisitions should be housed singly and kept away from any other reptiles in your possession for at least three months. This is preferably done in a separate room, and supplies should not be shared between quarantine animals and the rest of the collection. Always take care of isolated animals last, and sanitize your hands afterwards.

Quarantine allows for any potentially communicable problems to develop away from the main collection. The health of animals in quarantine should be closely monitored during this time. Some breeders administer dewormers or antiparasitic drugs as a preventative measure in case the snakes are harboring these organisms. However, deparasitizing should only be performed under the supervision of a veterinarian experienced with reptile medicine, because antiparasitic medications can be harmful to reptiles if administered improperly or when no parasites are actually present.

Captive-born animals are often considered to be free of parasites. This doesn't mean that the quarantine process can be skipped. Housing these "clean" animals in close proximity to wild-caught or otherwise sick animals (as is the case at some pet stores) greatly increases the risk of a captive-bred animal contracting a serious illness. In short, never skip the quarantine period, regardless of the source of your boa.

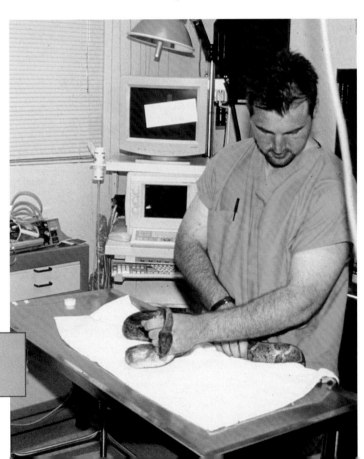

It is important to establish a relationship with a reptile veterinarian before an emergency crops up.

Shedding Problems

Dysecdysis is the inability to shed some or all of the skin, which can lead to other serious problems. Initially, a snake with a retained shed may no longer have the milky coloration a shedding snake normally displays, and the skin will usually have a dull, somewhat wrinkled appearance. The skin may be flaking off in areas, yet difficult to manually peel off. A snake with retained skin all over its body will be unlikely to eat until the skin has been removed. It may also display an inability to move naturally. An affected snake that is left untreated can become fatally ill.

Eyes and Tails

Sometimes the skin will be successfully shed on the body, but will be retained on the tail tip. If not caught in time, the skin may tighten and constrict the tail, restricting blood flow to the extremity and resulting in loss of the tail tip. This part of the body should always be checked after your snake has shed.

Snakes have a layer of skin over their eyes that is shed off, and often this eye cap (also called the *brille* or *spectacle*) is retained over the eye after shedding. After your snake sheds, you should always inspect its eyes (or the shed skin) to make sure the eye cap was shed off. If the eye cap is retained, the eye will appear dull or discolored, or it may have a slightly wrinkled appearance, or in some cases you may be able to see the edge of the eye cap slightly separated from the eye itself.

If caught early, removal is easily done by holding the snake's head and body securely, and using the sticky side of a piece of tape. Gently and lightly press the tape against the eye cap, and carefully pull the piece of skin away. If there is any difficulty in removing the eye cap, or if you are not comfortable doing this procedure, have your veterinarian do it for you. If a retained eye cap is left on too long, an infection can result, and the eye may become permanently damaged.

Causes and Remedies

Dysecdysis can be caused by a number of things, but most often it results from dehydration and/or low ambient humidity. Skin may also be retained at the site of a skin abrasion, bite, or burn. A variety of illnesses may result in a snake being unable to shed properly.

To treat dysecdysis, you will need to assess the condition of the snake first. If it is in advanced stages, veterinary aid may be necessary. If it is caught early, the problem can be corrected with no ill effects. Raise the humidity in the cage by misting the snake and inside of the cage. Add a large, shallow tray of water that the snake can soak in if it chooses. If the skin is flaking off, try to carefully peel the skin off, starting at the head and peeling back toward the tail. A small pair of forceps is helpful on juvenile snakes for removing bits of shed skin off the head. If the skin is left on too long, an infection can result between the old outer layer and the underlying layers of new skin, which will make removal difficult. Veterinary intervention is necessary as soon as possible to prevent the possible death of the snake.

Shedding problems are usually caused by low humidity and dehydration. The wrinkled skin of this boa is also a sign of dehydration.

External Injuries

External injuries such as skin lacerations and rodent bites usually heal without any problems as long as the cage is kept clean to prevent conditions that can lead to infection. Injuries should be monitored closely, and if infections appear, you should see your veterinarian. Topical antibiotic cream or ointment can be sparingly used on injuries as a precaution against infection. Apply the cream to the affected area, and then lightly wipe off any excess. Avoid using liberal amounts of antibiotic cream on injuries.

Parasites

Imported animals often have parasites that should be diagnosed and treated by a veterinarian. However, parasites are known to all animals and come in two general types: those that live on the outside of the body (ectoparasites) and those that live within the host body (endoparasites). Parasites are present in most organisms and normally remain at acceptable, non-harmful levels in animals that have a healthy immune system. When an animal becomes stressed, its immune system may not be functioning to its fullest healthy level, allowing the opportunity for the parasites to multiply and overtake the already weakened animal, possibly resulting in its death. Additionally, because many captive reptiles are in contact with their infested fecal material, they continuously reinfect themselves.

Internal Parasites

Any animal suffering from endoparasites may stop eating and become anorexic. Other symptoms include regurgitation of partially digested food and soft feces that smell worse than usual and may be grayish in color. Before your animal gets to this point, you should keep a keen eye out for any unusual behaviors so you may be able to avoid dire consequences.

Maintaining proper husbandry and appropriate habitat conditions are a must. The ambient temperature of your boa's enclosure should range from the low 80s to the mid-90s (26.7 to 35°C). This normal daytime temperature is essential for proper immune system function and therefore protection from disease and parasites that can debilitate an unhealthy reptile. It is for this same reason that boas often come down with respiratory illnesses, another common malady, when cooled during their prebreeding periods. Snakes may subsequently succumb to these and other afflictions unless returned to and kept in proper temperatures.

Analyzing a fresh fecal sample under a microscope will detect the presence of internal parasites. This is a job best left to an experienced veterinarian. Rarely will a fecal sample from any captive reptile be perfectly devoid of any microorganisms. There are normal populations of bacteria and protozoans that live within the bodies of reptiles, some of which are beneficial and aid in digestion, while others are parasitic yet are maintained at harmless levels by the immune system. Some inexperienced veterinarians want to treat a reptile for anything noticed in a fecal sample. Some antibiotics are harsh on the body, and improper dosages can cause death. An experienced reptile veterinarian will properly identify unhealthy levels of parasitic microorganisms and will be familiar with the best methods of treatment. There are disagreements in the developing field of herpetological medicine, and additional research is necessary to understand and better treat a number of common reptile parasites.

Flagellated Protozoans Various species of protozoans that move by means of a whip-like structure called a flagellum may be present in the feces of any reptile, especially imported reptiles. Though a small number present in a fecal sample is considered normal, a large

Heat Will Help

If an animal is sick, keep the temperature in its enclosure slightly higher than usual, as this has the same effect a fever does in warm-blooded animals—it creates an environment that is hostile to pathogens but is beneficial to the immune system.

Weight Loss

Snakes will often respond to stress or sickness by not eating, or chronic regurgitation may result, both of which will lead to weight loss if the problem is not corrected. Internal parasites can also cause emaciation. Usually the first signs of emaciation are when the backbone protrudes, creating a ridge down the snake's back. Underfeeding your snake can also result in emaciation. Seek veterinary attention if your boa ever suffers unexplained weight loss.

number can be harmful. Imported reptiles usually have high loads of protozoans, as the stress from the rigors of shipping compromises the animal's natural defenses, allowing the parasites to proliferate. Fortunately, when caught early, most flagellated protozoans are easily treated by your vet with drugs such as metronidazole. During the medication process, it is vital that the cage be thoroughly cleaned on at least a daily basis, but especially when you notice feces in the cage. If your snake is coming in contact with its feces, there is a good chance it will be reinfected.

Amoebiasis Amoebiasis, or amoebic dysentery, is a serious protozoan infection caused by the protozoan *Entamoeba invadens*. These amoebas ravage the digestive tract, eventually entering the bloodstream and spreading to other organs. Symptoms include diarrhea, refusal to eat, regurgitation, the urge to drink frequently, and stretching out the body in discomfort. If not immediately diagnosed and treated in its early stages, death can occur within a few weeks. Strict quarantine procedures should be put into effect to prevent spreading this highly infectious disease to other animals.

Cryptosporidiosis Cryptosporidiosis, an insidious protozoal disease that can pass from one host to another, cannot be treated. It is caused by *Cryptosporidium sp.* An animal diagnosed with this parasitic infection should never be placed with other boas. Never use furnishings or other supplies that have come in contact with infected reptiles with healthy animals.

This parasite lives in the digestive system, and during part of its life cycle it encases itself in the lining of the stomach and/or intestine, and large infestations can severely inflame these organs and disrupt digestion, ultimately leading to death. *Cryptosporidium* infections are one of the most feared diseases of reptiles. Cryptosporidiosis in reptiles may possibly be stress induced, though little research has been done to better understand this parasite.

The symptoms of cryptosporidiosis infection are usually regurgitation and weight loss, along with a prominent mid-body swelling, which is caused by the severely inflamed stomach lining. It is important to note that an animal carrying the disease may not show any signs of the illness for a long time. Infections can be diagnosed through fecal exams by an experienced vet before any outward symptoms are present, though snakes with *Cryptosporidium* present in their systems may not always be shedding evidence of parasites in their feces, making this an unreliable means of early detection.

This boa suffered a severe rat bite to its face. This is a graphic example of why you shoud feed only prekilled prey.

Once it becomes clear that a snake is infected, there is usually irreversible damage to the lining of the digestive tract that will eventually result in death. Because of the cost of caring for an animal with this disease, along with its suffering, euthanasia may be recommended.

Though currently untreatable, research is underway with at least one medication that will hopefully prove to be a means of preventing cryptosporidiosis from killing reptiles.

Worms Parasitic worms are sometimes found in the digestive tract of various reptiles in captivity, especially imported individuals. Sometimes, worms or their eggs might be clearly visible in your snake's feces. An experienced veterinarian can determine the presence of worms by analyzing fecal samples or other methods and can treat them with antibiotics.

Ectoparasites

By far, the two most common ectoparasites are mites and ticks. Both are small arachnids that bite snakes and drink their blood. While ticks are easy to see and eliminate, mites are far more insidious. Quarantining of newly acquired boas will help prevent the disastrous introduction of mites or ticks to your collection.

Mites The black snake mite, *Ophionyssus natricis*, is the most dreaded external parasite of boas because infestations can be spread easily, are difficult to control, and can cause extreme discomfort and even kill reptiles in serious cases. This blood-sucking species of mite usually

Veterinary Mite Treatment

If you can't eliminate mites yourself, or you want some professional help, contact your reptile veterinarian. He or she is likely to prescribe a solution of ivermectin to spray onto your snake and its enclosure. This medication is often used to eliminate heartworms in dogs. Follow your vet's instructions for using this product. If you keep any species of turtle, keep ivermectin away from them; this drug is highly toxic to most species of turtle.

affects snakes and large scaled lizards such as blue-tongue skinks. This species can multiply rapidly, often appearing to cover a snake almost overnight. Usually, mites become noticeable a few weeks or months after bringing a new snake into your home. All it takes is one female mite to create thousands in a short period of time. Control must occur immediately upon noticing mites on your animal. These mites can travel fairly long distances quite quickly, so they can soon infest all snakes in your home.

There are several methods to eliminate mites on your snake. Some breeders prefer to soak their snake in a tub of warm water to dislodge many of the mites, and then rub the snake down with a towel soaked with olive oil. Most remaining mites will stick to the oil-soaked towel. This will remove the majority of the mites, but not all of them. Often, mites will hide under larger scales such as those on the head, and especially in the groove around the edges of the eye cap, making removal difficult.

In addition to treating the snake, the entire cage and possibly the entire room will have mites present and will need treatment. If other snakes are nearby, you should treat them as if they have mites. At least one product that is sold in an aerosol can claims to be an effective method for treating mites on reptiles and their supplies. Opinions and experiences vary with regard to its safety around reptiles, so use it with caution and follow the directions closely. You can also treat the cage by throwing all organic materials (bedding, wooden climbing branches, etc.) away and soaking the cage and other fixtures in a 10 percent solution of bleach and water for 30 minutes or more. Rinse everything thoroughly. Because mite eggs are resilient and can be laid in the tiniest of crannies, you may need to treat the cage and snake again in a week or two.

Some importers use 10 percent Sevin dust sprinkled on the substrate as well as directly on the snake's body (away from the head) as an effective means of mite elimination. There are potential hazards with Sevin dust, and the manufacturer specifies that it is not for use on animals, so use of this product can be considered risky, but it is worth noting that some

This Peruvian boa is very thin. Parasitic infestations can cause weight loss and appetite suppression.

large reptile businesses have used it on a very large scale for years without any ill effects. Caution should be used as this dust can be caustic, as it is really a pesticide that also works as a medication in small dosages. Each state regulates the use of this substance, so check with your state Department of Agriculture. Zimermectin can be used to remove mites from your reptiles as well, and you can purchase this medication from your veterinarian.

Shedding is a snakes' natural defense against external parasites, and a snake with a mite infestation will be shedding very frequently. If you notice your infected snake about to shed, it is recommended to immediately discard the shed skin outside, promptly disinfect the snake's cage, and wipe down the snake with olive oil. The sooner you can do this after the snake sheds, the fewer mites will be able to recolonize on it.

There is unfortunately no simple, quick way to rid your snake of mites, as they will be present in the room the snake is in. A continuous effort of cleaning the snake and cage of mites will result in the gradual elimination of the parasites. Do not consider your snake free of mites until several months have passed without any mites seen upon close scrutiny.

Some types of mites you may see on your snake are harmless and not bloodsucking, and they only live on dead skin; these are thought to originate from wood chips, mulch, and even feeder mice. These harmless mites are usually light in color, contrasting greatly with the feared black snake mites. Regardless, any species of mite should not be allowed to persist and should be controlled by using the above methods.

Ticks Reptile ticks of the genus *Amblyomma* are another blood-sucking parasite commonly found on recently imported boas. Due to their large size, they are usually easy to notice and remove, and they don't reproduce at the same rate as snake mites. They disseminate disease into the host's bloodstream. Many ticks carry and harbor *Haemogregarina*, a blood trypanosome equated with "reptile malaria"—*Haemogregarina* does cause up to a 25 percent drop in hemoglobin levels in reptiles (Schall, 1982).

To successfully remove ticks, take a pair of tweezers, and by gently pulling on the head (usually hidden under one of the snake's scales), remove the entire tick and place it in alcohol where it may promptly die. Be careful to extract the head with the rest of the tick's body, as an infection may result if the head is left buried in the skin. Fortunately, ticks are much easier to control than mites, since they are larger and therefore easy to notice early and remove.

Inclusion Body Disease

Inclusion body disease (IBD) is a much-feared disease affecting primarily boas and pythons. IBD is caused by a virus, and the infection becomes systemic, affecting all major organs of the body. Clinical signs in affected snakes include chronic regurgitation and a variety of neurological disorders. The inability of the animals to right themselves when placed on their back, pointing the head upwards continuously (often called "stargazing"), head tremors, disorientation, and lack of coordination also occur. Animals showing symptoms of IBD should immediately be quarantined.

It is thought that some snakes may be carriers of this virus, yet never show clinical symptoms. These carriers may infect other snakes in a collection that don't show the same degree of immunity. A carrier might show symptoms if its immune system is compromised through poor husbandry conditions or other forms of stress.

Unfortunately, this disease is not treatable, and euthanization is necessary to avoid any continued pain and suffering. For anyone keeping more than one boa, it is advisable to treat all snakes like they are potential carriers of the disease. Sanitation of hands and supplies during contact with other snakes is necessary to help prevent the spread of IBD.

There are other viruses that affect boas and other reptiles, but little information exists on treatment, identification, and transmission. Diagnosis is possible only by a competent reptile veterinarian; so if you suspect a viral problem in your snake, notify your vet immediately.

Difficulty Giving Birth

When a female is unable to give birth to her babies, this is known as dystocia. This is similar to egg binding in egg-laying reptiles. The causes of dystocia are poorly known, but often attributed to nutritional deficiencies, lack of exercise, improper body weight, or internal defects. Baby boas retained in the mothers' body will die and decompose, causing internal infections. Dystocia is diagnosed when a gravid boa is past due and is showing a pronounced swelling in the abdomen. Sometimes, a female will successfully give birth to nearly all of her litter, but one or more may be retained in her body, which will also appear as a swelling. Surgical removal has been performed successfully, but the babies will most likely not survive the procedure. Your vet may also administer drugs to aid in the delivery process, and in some cases manual palpation can be used for removal. As soon as dystocia is suspected, immediately take your animal to the vet, as the condition can be fatal if left untreated for too long.

If your boa becomes ill, it will have the best chance of recovery if you seek veterinary attention sooner rather than later.

Prolapse of the Cloaca

The passing of the rear portion of the intestine outside the body is something that happens from time to time with reptiles and can occur for a number of reasons, some of which are not fully understood. Dystocia in females trying to pass eggs can sometimes end up prolapsing their cloaca. Intestinal impaction and abdominal injury can also create this problem, and other times there is no apparent cause. Consult with your veterinarian as soon as possible should your boa experience this problem. Surgery is usually required to remedy a cloacal prolapse.

Prolapse of the Hemipenis

Occasionally, a male boa will be unable to withdraw one of his two hemipenes back into his body after copulation. Sometimes this can be due to a piece of cage substrate other foreign material getting stuck to the organ preventing it from retracting, while other times there is no clear cause.

If caught early, the hemipenis can sometimes be massaged back into the base of the tail by experienced breeders. This is difficult to accomplish, and may not always be completely successful

Lack of a proper hiding place is one of many things that can cause your boa stress.

depending on how long the hemipenis has been prolapsed. Often the problem is caught after the hemipenis becomes necrotic, and it must be amputated by a veterinarian. A male missing one hemipenis can still mate and sire offspring.

Stress

As with humans, stress in reptiles can result from any uncomfortable experiences. By meeting all the requirements needed by red-tailed boas, problems with stress should not be an issue. Though your boa may not show it, you should assume that certain unavoidable events, like handling, are stressful to some degree. It is the owner's responsibility to make sure these uncomfortable times are kept to a minimum, and that the snake is kept happy by providing all that it needs for a healthy existence. Negative situations that continue for a long period of time will lead to health problems such as loss of appetite and a depressed immune system, which in turn can progress to more serious and possibly fatal problems.

Obesity

Obesity is usually a problem only with nonbreeding, well-fed animals. The snake will obviously appear plump, and the light colored skin between the scales will be clearly visible as the skin is stretched out. Close monitoring of your snake's weight and adjustment of feeding frequency or size of the offering will help prevent obesity.

Regurgitation

Regurgitation can occur as a result of rough handling (especially soon after feeding), extreme temperature changes after feeding, internal parasites, disease, or any stressful

Dehydration

Dehydration usually occurs due to neglect. As long as a boa is offered water and proper humidity levels, dehydration should not be an issue. Boas weakened from sickness or injury may not actively seek out water, and therefore may need to be offered water by bringing the bowl to the snake and gently directing the snake's head to the water's surface. Check the water bowl daily, always provide clean water, and never let a water bowl dry out.

situation. Always make sure you provide the correct warmth when your snake is digesting. See your vet if regurgitation occurs with any frequency.

Diarrhea

Liquefied feces may be one of the first signs that something is wrong with your snake. There can be many causes of diarrhea, so it is best to see your vet as soon as possible if your snake is having abnormal feces. Diarrhea will cause dehydration rapidly, so do not wait to seek treatment.

Intestinal Impactions

Large indigestible objects, or an accumulation of small indigestible objects, can become lodged in the intestine, restricting flow of waste and ultimately causing death if not passed. Occasionally, boas may get a mouthful of substrate when they are swallowing their food. Avoid feeding snakes on wood chips or other granular substrates.

Impactions may be clearly felt through the abdomen if the ingested object(s) are fairly large, but unfortunately most impactions are not noticed until a necropsy is performed to determine the cause of death.

Death and Euthanization

Should a death occur among your snakes, you should always do your best to determine the cause, especially if you own other animals that could be at risk. A fresh-dead snake should be examined all over to see if there are any clues to its demise. Things to look for include skin tears, shedding problems, blood or bloody feces in the cage, etc. Feel the abdomen for hard objects that may indicate an impaction. Try to find out if anyone used any toxic chemicals in the vicinity of your reptiles. Make sure to thoroughly wash your hands before touching any other animals.

A dark blue-green dot on the belly, appearing as if the skin has been stained, usually appears several hours after death. This dot is really just the bile leaking out of the gall bladder and absorbing into adjacent tissue, which is one of the earliest indications that decomposition has set in. It is not an indicator for the cause of death.

A snake in the process of dying will sometimes open and close its mouth, and often it will get a mouthful of substrate. Some keepers who find their dead snake with substrate in its mouth may jump to the conclusion that it died due to ingestion of the substrate, but this is normally not the case.

It is obviously upsetting to lose a pet. It is even more upsetting to have to make the decision to euthanize a favorite reptile that has no hope for recovery. A snake with a terminal ailment should be humanely euthanized by a veterinarian before it unnecessarily suffers too much.

Necropsy

If you have an animal mysteriously die, you may want to know what happened. This is especially important if the boa was kept in close proximity to other reptiles that could possibly be at risk. If there are no clear external reasons for the death, and it is obviously not due to poor care on your part, then having your vet perform a necropsy is an option. A necropsy is a dissection of the animal to analyze its internal structures for abnormalities in search of the cause of death.

The best subjects will be as fresh as possible. Since you should at least check up on your animals daily, you will notice when one dies. Immediately remove it from the cage and refrigerate it in an airtight plastic bag until you can deliver it to your vet. Do not freeze the boa, as this may damage cellular structure and make diagnosis difficult in some circumstances. The chances of determining the cause of death is reduced with animals that are showing early stages of decomposition, yet prominent problems like impactions will still be easily seen.

Often, everything will visually appear normal, yet your vet may suggest having organ samples examined by a histopathologist, who will look for viruses, bacteria, and other pathogens on a cellular level. This is costly, yet a worthy investment if you have a large colony of reptiles that you want to protect.

References

Andrews, Iain. 1996. The Care and Maintenance of the Common Boa. *Reptilian Magazine* 4(6):26-31.

Baker, Michael R. 1987. Synopsis of the Nematoda Parasitic in Amphibians and Reptiles. Memorial University of Newfoundland, *Occasional Papers in Biology* 11:1-325p.

Baltosser, William H. 1982. *Boa Constrictor imperator* (Boa Constrictor). Mexico, Sonora. *Herpetological Review* 13(3):81-82.

Barbour, Thomas. 1906. Reptilia and Amphibia. pp224-229. In: "*Vertebrata* from the Savanna of Panama" By Outram Bangs. *Bulletin of the Museum of Comparative Zoology* 46(12):223-230.

Barbour, Thomas and A.D. Amaral. 1924. Notes on some Central American Snakes. *Occasional Papers of the Boston Society of Natural History* 5:129-132.

Barker, Dave and T. 1994. Boas in the Spotlight. *The Vivarium*, September/October, 6(2):38-41.

Bartlett, A.D. 1894. On a singular case of one snake swallowing another in the Society's Reptile House. *Proceedings of the Zoological Society London*:669-670.

Bartlett, R.D. and P. Bartlett. 2003. *Florida's Snakes*. A Guide to their identification and habits. University Press of Florida, Gainesville. 182p.

Bayless, Mark K. 2003. Succesful Breeding of the Arabian Sand Boa. *Reptiles*, February, 11(2):6.

Beebe, William. 1946. Field Notes on the Snakes of Kartabo, British Guiana, and Caripito, Venezuela. *Zoologica* (N.Y.) 31(4):1-52 + PL. I-XIII.

Bertona, Miguel and M. Chiaraviglio. 2003. Reproductive Biology, Mating Aggregations, and Sexual Dimorphism of the Argentine Boa Constrictor (*Boa constrictor occidentalis*). *Journal of Herpetology* 37(3):510-516.

Boback, Scott M. 2004. *Boa constrictor* (Boa Constrictor). Diet. *Herpetological Review* 35(2):175.

Boback, Scott M., E. Burroughs, C. Ugarte, and J. Watling. 2000. *Boa Constrictor* (Boa Constrictor). Diet. *Herpetological Review* 31(4):244-245.

Bogert, Charles M. 1954. Book III: Amphibians and Reptiles of the World. pp1190-1390. IN: *Animal Kingdon* (Edited) Frederick Drimmer. Volume II. Greystone Press, New York. 1390p.

Bogert, Charles M. 1969. Boas – A Paradoxical Family. *Animal Kingdom* 72(4):19-25.

Bogert, Charles M. and J. A. Oliver. 1945. A Preliminary Analysis of the Herpetofauna of Sonora. *Bulletin of the American Museum of Natural History* 83(6):303-425.

Bowler, J.K. 1977. *Longevity of Reptiles and Amphibians in North American Collections.* S.S.A.R., Kansas. 32p.

Brattstrom, Bayard H. 1965. Body Temperatures of Reptiles. *The American Midland Naturalist*, April, 73(2):376-422.

Campbell, Jonathan A. 1998. *Amphibians and Reptiles of Northern Guatemala, The Yucatan, and Belize.* University of Oklahoma Press, Norman. 380p.

Carey, James R. 2003. *Longevity.* The Biology and Demography of life span. Princeton University Press, Princeton. 278p.

Carey, James R. and D.S. Judge. 2000. *Longevity Records: Life Spans of Mammals, Birds, Amphibians, Reptiles, and Fish.* Odense University Press, Odense (Denmark). Monographs on Population Aging 8:1-239.

Carlquist, Sherwin. 1965. *Island Life.* A Natural History of the Islands of the World. American Museum of Natural History, The Natural History Press, Garden City. 451p.

Casado, Roberto B. 1996. *Boa Constrictor Constrictor (Boa, Tragavenado). Herpetological Review* 27(2):88.

de Vosjoli, Philippe. 1990. *The General Care and Maintenance of Red-Tailed Boas.* The Herpetocultural Library, Series 200, Lakeside. 48p.

de Vosjoli, Philippe. 1997a. Ethnoherpetology: The Big Herp Crash of 1997 and the future of Herpetoculture. The *Vivarium*, September/October, 8(6):26-28, 66.

de Vosjoli, Philippe. 1997b. A New Look at *Boa Constrictors. The Vivarium*, December/January, 9(1):37-43.

Divers, Stephen. 1993. Captive husbandry of the Columbian *Boa Constrictor. Reptilian Magazine* 1(8):24-29.

Divers, Stephen J. 1996. Reproductive Biology and Reproductive Problems of Boas and Pythons. *Reptilian Magazine* 4(4):52-58.

Dowling, Herndon G. 1965. *Boa Constrictor:* From Tropical Menace to Popular Pet. *Animal Kingdom*, Nov.-Dec., 68(6):183-185.

Fogel, David. 1997. *Captive Propagation of the Boa Constrictors and Related Boas.* Krieger Publishing Co., Malabar. 98p.

Forcart, Lothar. 1951. Nomenclature Remarks on Some Generic Names of the Snake Family Boiidae. *Herpetologica* 7:197-199.

Greene, Harry W. 1978. Behavior and Phylogeny: Constriction in Ancient and Modern Snakes. *Science*, 07 April, 200(4337):74-77.

Greene, Harry W. 1983. *Boa Constrictor*. pp380-382. IN: *Costa Rican Natural History* (Edited) By Daniel H. Janzen. University of Chicago Press, Chicago. 816p.

Henderson, Robert W. and R. Powell (Editors). 2003. *Islands and the Sea*. Essays on Herpetological Exploration in the West Indies. S.S.A.R., Salt Lake City, Utah. 304p.

Henderson, Robert W., T.W. Micucci, G. Puorto, and R.W. Bourgeois. 1995. Ecological correlates and patterns in the distribution of neotropical boines (Serpentes: Boidae): a preliminary assessment. *Herpetological Natural History* 3:15-27.

Herfs, A. 1959. Beutefang, Nahrungsaufnahme und Wachstum bei *Boa constrictor* (L.)[Capture of prey, food intake and growth in *Boa constrictor* (L.)]. *Acta-Tropica* 16(1):1-37.

Langhammer, James K. 1983. A New Subspecies of Boa Constrictor, *Boa constrictor melanogaster*, from Ecuador (Serpentes: Boidae). *Tropical Fish Hobbyist*, December, #334, 32(4):70-79.

Martinez-Morales, Miguel A. and A.D. Cuaron. 1999. *Boa constrictor*, an introduced predator threatening the endemic fauna on Cozumel Island, Mexico. *Biodiversity and Conservation* 8:957-963.

McGinnis, S.M. and R.G. Moore. 1969. Thermo-regulation in the boa constrictor *Boa constrictor*. *Herpetologica* 25:38-45.

Montgomery, Gene G. and A.S. Rand. 1978. Movements, Body Temperature and Hunting Strategy of a *Boa Constrictor*. *Copeia* 3:532-533.

Myres, Brian C. and M.M. Eells. 1968. Thermal Aggregation in *Boa Constrictor*. *Herpetologica* 24(1):61-66.

Neill, Wilfred T. 1958. The occurrence of amphibians and reptiles in saltwater areas, and a bibliography. *Bulletin of the Marine Science Gulf and Caribbean* 8(1):1-97.

Neill, Wilfred T. 1962a. The Reproductive Cycle of Snakes in a Tropical Region, British Honduras. *Quarterly Journal of the Florida Academy of Sciences*, 25(3):234-253.

Neill, Wilfred T. and R. Allen. 1962b. Reptiles of the Cambridge Expedition to British Honduras, 1959-60. *Herpetologica* 18(2):79-91.

Peters, James A. and B. Orejas-Miranda. 1970. *Catalogue of the Neotropical Squamata Part I: Snakes*. Volume I – II. United States National Museum Bulletin 297. Smithsonian Institution Press, Washington, D.C. 293p.

Peters, James A. and B. Orejas-Miranda. 1986. *Catalogue of the Neotropical Squamata*. Part I: Snakes. pp1-337. Smithsonian Institution Press, Washington, D.C. 640p.

Pope, Clifford H. 1961. *The Giant Snakes*. Alfred A. Knopf, New York. 296p.

Quick, John S., H.K. Reinert, E.R. de Cuba, and R.A. Odum. 2005. Recent Occurrence and Dietary Habits of *Boa Constrictor* on Aruba, Dutch West Indies. *Journal of Herpetology* 39(2):304-307.

Rivera, P.C., M. Chiaraviglio, G. Perez, and C.N. Gardeneal. 2005. Protein polymorphism in populations of *Boa constrictor occidentalis* (Boidae) from Cordoba province, Argentina. *Amphibia–Reptilia* 26:175-181.

Ronne, Jeff. 1996. Revelations of a Boa Breeder. *Reptiles*, November, 4(11):24-26, 28-32, 34, 36-38, 40, 42-43.

Ross, Richard A. [M.D.] and G. Marzec. 1990. *The Reproductive Husbandry of Pythons and Boas*. Institute for Herpetological Research, Stanford. 270p.

Russo, Vincent. 2004. "Mini" Boas. *Reptiles*, April, 12(4):44-59.

Sanderson, Ivan T. 1941. *Living Treasure*. The Viking Press, New York. 290p.

Sanderson, Ivan T. 1972. *Living Mammals of the World*. Doubleday and Company, Garden City. 303p.

Schall, Jos, J., A.F. Bennett, and R.W. Putnam. 1982. Lizards Infected with Malaria: Physiological and Behavioral Consequences. *Science*, 10 September, 217:1057-1059.

Schatzl, Kurt. 1995. Notes on the Breeding Common Boa Constrictors. *Reptile and Amphibian Magazine*, July/August, pp114-122.

Schmidt, Karl P. and W.F. Walker, Jr. 1943. Snakes of the Peruvian Coastal Region. *Zoological Series of the Field Museum of Natural History* 24(27):297-324.

Stull, Olive G. 1932. Five New Species of the Family Boidae. *Occasional Papers of the Boston Society of Natural History* 8:25-30 + PL 1-2.

Stull, Olive G. 1935. A Check List of the Family Boidae. *Proceedings of the Boston Society of Natural History* 40(8):387-408.

Taylor, Edward H. 1936. Notes on the Herpetological Fauna of the Mexican State of Sonora. *The University of Kansas Science Bulletin* 24(19):475-501.

Walls, Jerry G. 1998. *The Living Boas*. A complete guide to the Boas of the World. T.F.H. Publications, Neptune City. 288p.

Young, Bruce A. 1990. Is there a direct link between the ophidian tongue and Jacobson's Organ? *Amphibia-Reptilia* 11:263-276.

Zweifel, Richard G. 1960. Results of the Puritan-American Museum of Natural History Expedition to Western Mexico. 9. Herpetology of the Tres Marias Islands. *Bulletin of the American Museum of Natural History* 119(2):77-128 + PL. 41-44.

Zweifel, Richard G. 1981. Genetics of color pattern polymorphism in the California King Snake. *Journal of Heredity* 72:238-244

CLUBS AND SOCIETIES

Amphibian, Reptile & Insect Association
Liz Price
23 Windmill Rd
Irthlingsborough
Wellingborough NN9 5RJ
England

American Society of Ichthyologists and Herpetologists
Maureen Donnelly, Secretary
Grice Marine Laboratory
Florida International University
Biological Sciences
11200 SW 8th St.
Miami, FL 33199
Telephone: (305) 348-1235
E-mail: asih@fiu.edu
www.asih.org

Society for the Study of Amphibians and Reptiles (SSAR)
Marion Preest, Secretary
The Claremont Colleges
925 N. Mills Ave.
Claremont, CA 91711
Telephone: 909-607-8014
E-mail: mpreest@jsd.claremont.edu
www.ssarherps.org

VETERINARY RESOURCES

Association of Reptile and Amphibian Veterinarians (ARAV)
P.O. Box 605
Chester Heights, PA 19017
Phone: 610-358-9530
Fax: 610-892-4813
E-mail: ARAVETS@aol.com
www.arav.org

RESCUE AND ADOPTION SERVICES

ASPCA
424 East 92nd Street
New York, NY 10128-6801
Phone: (212) 876-7700
E-mail: information@aspca.org
www.aspca.org

New England Amphibian and Reptile Rescue
www.nearr.com

Petfinder.com
www.petfinder.org

Reptile Rescue, Canada
http://www.reptilerescue.on.ca

RSPCA (UK)
Wilberforce Way
Southwater

Horsham, West Sussex RH13 9RS
Telephone: 0870 3335 999
www.rspca.org.uk

WEBSITES

Federation of British Herpetologists
www.F-B-H.co.uk

Herp Station
http://www.petstation.com/herps.html

Kingsnake.com
http://www.kingsnake.com

Melissa Kaplan's Herp Care Collection
http://www.anapsid.org/boa.html

Red Tail Boa Community Forum
http://www.redtailboas.com/

RedTailBoa FAQ
http://www.redtailboafaq.com

Redtailboa.net
http://redtailboa.net/

Reptile Forums
http://reptileforums.com/forums/

Reptile Rooms, The
http://www.reptilerooms.org

MAGAZINES

Herp Digest
www.herpdigest.org

Reptiles Magazine
P.O. Box 6050
Mission Viejo, CA 92690
www.animalnetwork.com/reptiles

Reptilia Magazine
Salvador Mundi 2
Spain-08017 Barcelona
Subscripciones-subscriptions@reptilia.org

Photo Credits:

Randall Babb: 29
Marian Bacon: 46
R. D. Bartlett: 1, 11, 14, 22, 25, 28, 56, 60, 67, 85, 111, 114
Adam Black (Courtesy of Mike Layman): 26, 31, 33, 35, 38, 78, 82, 87, 96
Adam Black (Courtesy of Ophiological Services): 98
Allen Both: 6, 53
Isabelle Francais: 4, 50, 55, 58, 63 74, 76, 102, 106
Paul Freed: 16, 70, 109
M. & M. Kennedy: 89, 91, 93
J. K. Langhammer: 20
Erik Loza: 24,
W. P. Mara: 45
G. & C. Merker: 3, 48, 68, 96, and front cover
Jim Merli: 19, 65
Gerald L. Moore: 40
John Peelle: 104, 113
Mark Smith: 61, 100
K. H. Switak: 36, 71, 80
Zoltan Takacs: 8
John C. Tyson: 43, and back cover

Index

Note: boldface numbers indicate illustrations; a t indicates a table.

acclimatizing your new boa, 45
age, size, and cage requirements, 61–65
aggregative behavior, 33
aggression, 22, 33–34, 39
alleles, 92
Amaral's boa. *See Boa constrictor amarali*
amelanistic (albino) boa, **33**, **46**, **61**, 93, **94**, 95–96
amoebiasis, 108
anaconda. *See Eunectes sp.*
anal scales, 12
anerythrism, 96
arboreal boas, 16–17
Argentine boa. *See Boa constrictor occidentalis*
attacking prey, 34–35

Barbour, Thomas, 21, 25
Beebe, William, 79
behavior of boa, 31–32
birthing problems (dystocia), 113
bite wound, **109**
biting, 33–34, 66–67
black-bellied boas, **20**
bloodlines, 95
Boa constrictor amarali (Amaral's boa; Bolivian boa; short-tailed boa; spectacled boa), 14, 16, **16**
 life span and longevity, 27t
 range of, 13t
 record size for, 21t
Boa constrictor constrictor (red-tailed boa), 12–13, **14**
 life span and longevity, 27t
 range of, 13t
 record size for, 21t
Boa constrictor imperator (Central American boa; Colombian boa; Mexican boa; northern boa), 15–17, **19**
 life span and longevity, 27t
 range of, 13t

record size for, 21t
Boa constrictor longicauda (Long-tailed boa), 17–19
 range of, 13t
Boa constrictor melanogaster, 19
 range of, 13t
Boa constrictor nebulosus (Clouded boa; Dominican boa), 20, **21**
 range of, 13t
 record size for, 21t
Boa constrictor occidentalis (Argentine boa), 10, 11, 14, 20–21, **67**
 range of, 13t
 record size for, 21t
Boa constrictor orophias (Tete-Chien or dog's-head boa), 23
 record size for, 21t
Boa constrictor ortonii, 24, **24**
 life span and longevity, 27t
 range of, 13t
 record size for, 21t
Boa constrictor sabogae (Taboga boa; Saboga boa), 25
 range of, 13t
 record size for, 21t
body temperatures, 17t
Boidae family, 8, 11
Bolivian boa. *See Boa constrictor amarali*
Boulenger, E.G., 4
Boulenger, George, 4
breeders, 43
breeding, 81–99
 birthing problems (dystocia) and, 113
 bloodlines in, 95
 brooding chambers and, 89
 cages and housing for, 82
 codominant traits in, 96–97
 conditioning animals before, 88
 dominant genetic traits and, 93
 gestation period following, 90
 litter size in, 91
 live-bearing in, 8

124 *Red-Tailed Boas*